Boiling Point 2017

Woe, Woe, Woe to the Inhabitants of Earth, an End Times Prediction

Richard Denis

WestBow
PRESS

Copyright © 2012 Richard Denis

All rights reserved. No part of this book may be used or reproduced by any means, graphic, electronic, or mechanical, including photocopying, recording, taping or by any information storage retrieval system without the written permission of the publisher except in the case of brief quotations embodied in critical articles and reviews.

WestBow Press books may be ordered through booksellers or by contacting:

WestBow Press
A Division of Thomas Nelson
1663 Liberty Drive
Bloomington, IN 47403
www.westbowpress.com
1-(866) 928-1240

Because of the dynamic nature of the Internet, any web addresses or links contained in this book may have changed since publication and may no longer be valid. The views expressed in this work are solely those of the author and do not necessarily reflect the views of the publisher, and the publisher hereby disclaims any responsibility for them.

Any people depicted in stock imagery provided by Thinkstock are models, and such images are being used for illustrative purposes only.

Certain stock imagery © Thinkstock.

Scripture quotations taken from the New American Standard Bible®, Copyright © 1960, 1962, 1963, 1968, 1971, 1972, 1973, 1975, 1977, 1995 by The Lockman Foundation. Used by permission." (www.Lockman.org)

ISBN: 978-1-4497-3075-8 (sc)
ISBN: 978-1-4497-3076-5 (e)

Library of Congress Control Number: 2011960165

Printed in the United States of America

WestBow Press rev. date: 05/29/2012

Acknowledgements

I want to thank God, Jesus, the Holy Spirit, and the Blessed Virgin Mary for their inspiration, guidance, and patience with me.

In Memoriam

Gus & Mary Denis

Dedication

To my wife Vicki, daughters Destiny and Lindsey,
My sisters Connie, Karen, Nancy
And my brother Ted

Table of Contents

Chapter 1:   The Season Is Near 1
Chapter 2:   Satan: (The Final Enemy of Mankind) 7
Chapter 3:   A Time for Reaping 12
Chapter 4:   An Era of Change 19
Chapter 5:   A World Fallen Into Social Decay 38
Chapter 6:   A World Fallen Into Moral Decay 61
Chapter 7:   A World in Chaos 74
Chapter 8:   A World Lead by Evil Men 79
Chapter 9:   Signs upon the Earth 86
Chapter 10: A Flood of Knowledge in Our Time 98
Chapter 11: The Beginning to the End 102
Chapter 12: Seers 105
Chapter 13: Prophecy 119
Chapter 14: Visions (The Beginning of the Sorrows:
             1910-1940) 126
Chapter 15: Visions (The Pot of Water is on the Stove: 1940s) ... 140
Chapter 16: Visions (The Water is Warming: 1950-70s) 147
Chapter 17: Visions (The Water Is Getting Hot: 1980-2000s) 161
Chapter 18: Visions (The Water Is Boiling) 177
Chapter 19: Tears 185

Prologue i

This book is written for the reader to try to comprehend that the end of the world was known to God before the Earth was formed. Every event, every person in history served in some way to bring this time in our history to this special moment. Attempts will be made to show how some of these cumulative events, which have happened in the past century, are bringing our planet closer to its end, and at the same time, to its new beginning.

Many of our actions have hastened us to reach our current perilous end times. Most especially, as we had passed through the twentieth century, large numbers of humanity have been degenerating into a mass of demonic worshiping beings. Each of the past ten decades of the twentieth century will be scrutinized for every significant incident that has systematically led mankind on a slow, but methodical abandonment of God.

The actual data collected and presented in this book will provide the reader with an in-depth understanding that the stability of the world, both through nature and human actions, is at a precarious state. All that exists as we know it will be ending in our lifetimes as a result of our desire to want to put aside God's commandments in our lives.

In addition to the facts forewarning of Earth's waning moments, there will be a review of prophets and civilizations that spoke of the current conditions required for this period of time to come its decided ending. In addition, there are chapters dedicated to all those visionaries, selected by God, who have been permitted to both see and communicate with the Virgin Mary. The Mother of God has frequently given messages for all peoples, all faiths, and all ideologies of the world. Currently, she is warning humanity to listen to her messengers and live the messages that she has given to them. The messages are simply to convert, love, forgiving others, and seek reconciliation from God.

It is also important for the reader; especially those of non-Catholic faith, to read with an open mind. They must remember God speaks to everyone and has specifically provided each faith and Christian denomination with selected individuals to deliver His messages (i.e. Billy Graham). If one elects to close one's mind regarding messages given by God to certain individuals', particular of other denominations, then they may not receive the entire message and in essence are denying that God has the right to choose anyone to be His voice on earth.

Here is a fictional story about three men who were on a boat. The three men were standing on the top deck of a boat when a large wave pushed the boat sideways so much that they all fell overboard. One man, who was a Muslim cried out, "Allah, please help me." Well, a young man on the boat heard his cry for help, so he threw him a rope, but the Muslim man refused to take it, and drowned. The other man, a Protestant, cried out, "Oh Jesus, please help me." A young woman heard his plea and she threw him a rope, but he didn't take it, and drowned. The third man was a rather plump atheist, who overdulged in everything in life; he was panicking and was about to drown, but managed to cry out, "Oh God, please help me." An old man heard his plea and threw out a rope and the young man grabbed it and he was saved. Afterwards, when he was pulled safely aboard the boat, the young man said, "Thank God, you saved my life old man." The old man replied, "You're welcomed." Well, when the Protestant stood before God on judgment day, he said, "God, I cried out to Jesus to be saved from drowning, but He didn't help me. God replied, My Son Jesus was busy, so I had His mother Mary, throw you a rope, but you refused to take it. Likewise, the Muslim man also stood before God on judgment day and said, "Allah, I called out to you to save me from drowning, but you didn't do it". God replied, "I had my son Jesus throw you the rope instead, but you refused to take it; for you see it required both the Holy Spirit and I to save a man from drowning too".

The moral of the story is that God will choose anyone He wants to save someone from death. Generally men think they know who this individual should be, but they may end-up dying if they refuse to be helped by the one God has sent to them. Many Christian denominations refuse to acknowledge that Mary is someone who can help them to be saved. God has given Mary a rope in her hand to save people from dying, but many people refuse to take it because she is not the Holy Trinity. What makes people think that God wouldn't use every available resource at His command to save us from Satan? Therefore, let no one set in concrete an opinion that God will only chose someone from their own faith, or denomination to forewarn the world of Jesus's Second Coming; for by doing so, they ignore all other messengers that God provided to speak to His people in this time of crisis.

Prologue ii

We are in a war that surpasses any war in history, and the number of casualties could be in the billions. It is not a war of man vs. man, but rather a spiritual war with Satan. Satan is on a quest to destroy all of mankind, and to lead our souls into damnation where they will be his to rule forever. This war is real and many people do not even know that they are in battle with Satan. Nonetheless, he has been making tremendous gains in collecting souls throughout the twentieth century. However, as with any war, there will be a conclusion, and as Jesus pointed out in his parable (Matthew 13:24), "*the wheat and the tares will be separated at harvest time and the tares will be bundled and thrown into the fire to be burnt.*" Human beings are allowing themselves to be manipulated by demons, because they lack prayer and have lost their belief in an Almighty God, and therefore they may be thrown into the fire at harvest time (end times).

We live in a world, in which we give names to those individuals who are under Satan's influence. Psychologist refer to people who are calm one moment and angry the next minute, as being bi-polar, and others who are constantly raging and talking to themselves, as being schizophrenic. What these psychologists have done, by giving names for these symptoms, is to deny that some individuals are actually under demonic subjugation. In fact, there are biblical accounts of demonic possession. One such account, Mark (5:1), described Jesus encountering a man, who was raving and foaming at the mouth. Jesus called out the demon possessing this individual and asked by what named it was called, it responded "legion". As it turned out there were thousands of demons in this man.

In our society today, skeptics would say the man was probably an epileptic going through a seizure and Jesus did nothing but watch him recover from it. These skeptics are wrong, demons do exist, and they alter our behaviors in many ways. Homosexuality, cross-dressing, alcoholism, drug abuse, hatred, prejudice, anger, greed, sexual immorality, killing, physical and verbal abuses, lust, disobedience, etc., are all being caused by demonic forces. So, if we are being controlled by demons, how can any soul reach Heaven? Can anyone be saved?

All is not lost for humanity, the Virgin Mary says that through unceasing prayer (the armor of God) and fasting we can prevent demons from entering our minds and controlling us. Fasting is not based solely upon abstinence from food, but anything we that overly enjoy, which prevents us from worshipping God. However, many humans no longer pray or fast; thereby, enabling these demonic forces to permeate us with an overwhelming amount desire for lusts. These actions will eventually result in a world filled with so much chaos and hatefulness that God will be forced to destroy everything.

We are rapidly approaching this end time scenario, and the beginnings to the fulfillment of biblical end of the world prophecies are becoming more visible in our everyday lives. We are ignoring the many warnings God has given us: through the prophets, mystics, and especially the presence of the Blessed Virgin Mary, who has been seen throughout the world. The most well-known account for end of the world prophecies have been summarized in the Book of Revelation, written by John of Patmos. It contained much symbolism and brought into account those predictions from Ezekiel, Zechariah and Daniel. John describes a period in time, when there will be three and one-half years of peace, followed by three and one-half years of absolute destruction and chaos. He refers to the last days for humanity as the moment when the antichrist rules the Earth, and it will be a time of great despair.

During this time of hardship, there will be worldwide famines, plagues, wars, and death; all of which are happening in our world today. The events that will help fulfill the tribulation include: a mountain (asteroid) falling out of the sky and hitting the oceans, a great multitude of earthquakes, a world consumed by fires, the sun darkening, huge numbers of people dying through devastations, and even the stars appearing to roll up like a scroll. After all of this destruction, the Earth will be restored, and Jesus will live amongst his people for one thousand years

In the event that we are on this path of destruction, we need to evaluate our current moral values and determine if they coincide with God's law. If they do not, and instead we have fallen away from the truth, then the Second Coming of Jesus Christ may not be far off, and therefore all the suffering, as describe in the Book of Revelation, will shortly befall us.

Chapter 1

The Season Is Near

There have been a lot of television programs and books written, discussing that the end of the world will occur on December 21, 2012, as predicted by the Mayan Calendar. The Mayans calculated that all the planets in the solar system would not only be in a single line on this date, but they also would be directed towards the center of the Milky Way Galaxy. This alignment of the planets, which occurs once every 26000 years, would usher out the old world and herald in a new one. However, for those who believe that the world will end on this date are wrong.

Numerous New Testament references, as well, mention the last days of the world. The apostle writers of Matthew (24:29–44), Mark (13:24–31) and Luke (21:20–33) quoted Jesus as saying *"no one knows the hour or day when the world will end, but there will be many false prophets, the word of God would be preached throughout the world, there will be wars and rumors of wars and nations will rise against other nations."* Not only will those things take place, but there would also be famines, earthquakes, and it will be a time when the sun darkens and the stars will fall from the sky. This will all become a reality during the great tribulation, a period of trials.

Note that Jesus said, "no one knows the hour or day when this transpires", only the Father in Heaven knows. However, in Mark (13:28–29) Jesus also said, *"Learn a lesson from the fig tree. When its branch becomes tender and sprout leaves, you know that summer is near. In the same way, when you see that one can see these things happening, know that He is near, at the gates."* His statement suggests that if the fig leaves have already begun to sprout, then other outcomes have already been fulfilled; such as, winter would be over, the days would be getting longer, and Earth would be preparing for a new season of growth by providing necessary rains and the warmth of the sun. In a like manner, certain events must be fulfilled before the beginning of the end of time.

In general, many things must have been put in place before the initiation of this final occurrence. It is like putting a pot of water on a stove and turning up the heat. Initially, the water is cool and there is not much worth noticing, but when heat is applied to the water, it becomes warmer. After a while, the water will become so hot that it reaches its boiling point. Similarly, as we approach the end times the world will begin to experience some changes in ideologies, morale behavior, beliefs, faith, economics, governmental policies and climate alterations. The fabric of society will begin to show wear, and at first these transformations may not even appear to be noticeable. In fact, some people would say these are just aberrations from the norm; but in reality, as each year passes the frequency of these deviations will become increasingly greater and greater until absolute bedlam dominates the world.

Unlike the pot of water on the stove, which started off cool, no one knows when these changes in our current society began, and therefore when the final days will ultimately come upon mankind. However, there have been a couple of signs indicating this timeline may have already begun. The first sign was a vision, experienced by Pope Leo XIII on October 13, 1884. In that vision, Pope Leo XIII saw Satan boasting to God that he could destroy God's church if he was given sufficient time. According to Pope Leo XIII, God granted Satan one hundred years to try to do away with his church, but if Satan failed, he would be forever placed in Hell.

The beginning of Satan's one hundred year timeframe is unknown. However, an episode happened in May 13, 1917, which may more closely pinpoint to the beginning of it. At that time, in Fatima, Portugal, three young children named Lucia, Jacinta, and Francisco saw a vision of the Virgin Mary. However it wasn't until July 13, 1917, around noon, when the Mother of God entrusted these children with three secrets. In her message to them, the Virgin Mary warned them that the world was on a precipice of catastrophic times. Her first secret predicted that although World War I would come to an end, another more destructive war would start in the not-too-distant future under Pope Pius XII. Her second secret stated that if Russia was not consecrated to her immaculate heart by all the bishops of the world; then Russia would spread its errors throughout the world, and humanity would suffer greatly. Her third secret (recently released) indicated there would be a time when the pope and bishops would experience persecutions of the church, and there would be devastation of a city. Could this destruction of a city be possibly Rome, the very heart of Christianity, or could it be a metaphor for the destruction of Christianity and humanity itself?

Was this the reason why the Virgin Mary came down to Earth? Was it to prepare the world for its' last days? Was the year 1917, the beginning of the clock for Satan's one hundred years and the end of the world as we know it? If so, taking into account the hundred years that God granted Satan, and assuming Mary was also given one hundred years to prepare God's children for this period; she may have begun her warnings at about the same time that Satan began his campaign to wipe out God's church. Therefore, the end times may be in the year 2017, or alternately the year 2017 may represent only the beginning of the end times.

Examination of the Book of Revelation reveals that the end times cover a period of seven years. The seven years will be broken into two three and half year phases. The first phase will comprise three and half years of peace under the control of the antichrist, while the second three and half years will involve wars and numerous natural disasters before the Earth succumbs to its ultimate destruction. Under these circumstances, the last days of mankind would then be in the year 2024. In either scenario, the year 2017 is a very pivotal time period for mankind.

Satan has a plan to, once and for all, exterminate mankind's' relationship with God, and for us to follow him instead. One way for him to achieve this feat can be easily accomplished by controlling our human weaknesses. He has incredible power to influence us just by manipulating our minds. He will always persuade us to do something wrong. It is a war of attrition, one in which he will never give up. Therefore, no one should under estimate the power of Satan; he was after all an angel of God whose name was Lucifer. No one can see him, but we can see where he has been treading just by seeing large outbreaks of evil. When he finds a human's defenselessness towards an evil temptation, he will attempt to use it on everyone. If it is ineffective on an individual, Satan will switch to another tactic, and continually do so until he has found a weakness in everyone. He has found our shortcomings toward lust, power, and greed throughout generations after generations, and he has taken advantage of these temptations, with the result of many souls already fallen into damnation.

If Satan was given a hundred years to attempt to eradicate the church, what better time than the twentieth century was there for him to begin his campaign? Some old weapons at Satan's disposal have been hate, war, jealousy, vengeance, prejudice, racism, pride, disobedience, disrespect, laziness, arrogance, etc. His more recent weapons include drugs, knowledge, fame, modern day technologies; such as movies, Play Station-type games (this entertainment creates a lazy and overly aggressive society), mass communication via Internet or television, advance war machines, etc.

Satan's strategy is to utilize these newer inventions to modify the way we think and how we behave. He wants to alter our moral values and to sway the masses from acknowledging in the existence of God. He wants human beings to believe they are in control of their destiny and have the ability to create and destroy. If people accept this ideology, then humanity will no longer believe they have a need for God, and Satan will be victorious in achieving his domination over humanity.

One way for Satan to achieve his objective would be to fill us with rebellion and a sense of ultimate independence from God. Rebellion is the same strategy Satan used when he and one-third of God's holy angels sought to usurp the authority of God. Satan may have thought, "A war– yes, just like the one I started in Heaven; it is an excellent way to destroy humanity and lead their souls into damnation." He has been extremely successful imparting rebelliousness and war in the minds of human beings. The twentieth century was a violent time with two world wars (WWI and WWII), the Korean and Vietnam wars, Croatian-Serbian war, the Iraq and Afghanistan wars, and numerous other civil wars throughout the world that did not include NATO forces. There has been no peace at all in the twentieth century, and with all the new types of weaponry at our disposal, there is a great degree of unrest in our world.

In addition, the twentieth century has experienced an unprecedented amount of technological development. For example, technology in developed countries increased our lifespans through medical advances by means of heart, liver, and kidney transplants. We have also revised the way we travel throughout the world: fly in the skies in jet airplanes; travel under water in submarines, or upon the water with enormous ships, and we move upon the land in automobiles, or super-fast trains. We can go into outer space using rockets ships and build space stations with people living in them. Our technology has enabled us to make night into day; brought us pleasures of every sort; increased food production through genetic modification, and given us activities and games to entertain ourselves.

Our scientific accomplishments have made our lives easier but at a cost, for we have become lazy, complacent and have put ourselves on par with God. We no longer feel a need to be dependent upon Him, because we can solve anything with our understanding of the elements. Technology has become our god, and we believe that any supreme deity that cannot be seen is only a quaint artifact from long ago; created by our ancestors, who did not understand science.

One of God's commandments is *"Thou shalt not worship any other god."* Not only have we made our achievements our god, but we also have made baseball, football, soccer, basketball, and golf into our gods. We worship those individuals who perform best in these sports. We wear shirts with the names of our favorite players on them. We also worship rock stars, actors and actresses from afar and try to emulate them in the way we look, think, and behave. Indeed, the twentieth century was a perfect setting for Satan to begin his campaign against God; he has all the tools needed to twist our society into his evil likeness. How can anyone endure these days of Satan?

God knew mankind could not survive the temptations of Satan. Therefore, before any end of the world development could emerge, God needed a means to rescue humanity from Satan's grasp. His first step was to send His Son Jesus into the world. Jesus would be tempted by Satan, but would never succumb to him, and by dying on the cross without sin, He became the only means humanity could be saved from Satan's seductions. All that we would have to do, in order to be rescued from eternal damnation, is to ask God to be forgiven for our sins. This forgiveness is a grace given by God, as a result of Jesus's sacrifice on the cross; whether we are Christian, Jew, Muslim, Buddhist, atheists, etc. Without this grace from God all of humanity would perish to an eternal death.

Jesus was the first preparation by God to save humanity before end of the world, but it would still take another two thousand years before the actual fulfillment of this time would become a reality. And as it draws closer to the end, God will be providing many more signs that the Second Coming of Jesus is near. Included in these sign; are the unprecedented number of appearances of the Virgin Mary, who is being seen by many visionaries and other people throughout the world, and the return of the Jews to Israel, thereby fulfilling biblical prophecy of their presence in the Holy Land, a prerequisite for the final battle at Armageddon. Other signs consist of world instability with nations rising against nations, economic distress throughout the world, hatred growing among peoples, immorality, greed, and most importantly there will be humanities' indifference towards God. When we put all of these pieces together, we can see that we have begun an age unlike any other, and that the hand of God's justice may soon strike the world.

Chapter 2

Satan: (The Final Enemy of Mankind)

With every war there is a defined enemy. The enemy can be physically identified, and has an ideology opposite of its combatant. In order to defeat this opponent, one must overwhelm them with force until they are no longer able to continue their fight. Satan, however, is no ordinary enemy. He was an angel of God who has extraordinary powers; such as, those described in the Old Testament where one angel was able to destroy the entire Assyrian army. God had given all angels knowledge, and intellect that far exceeds that given to humans.

People don't believe in Satan because they cannot see him. Oh yes, Hollywood has depicted him several ways; one in which he is a red-colored cartoon character with horns and a tail, while other representations of Satan have been as a gruesome beast, or as a friend to mankind that can even look as a gorgeous woman (Elizabeth Hurley in the movie 'Bedazzled'). The only accurate depiction of Satan is that he is a ferocious creature seeking to devour human souls.

He is cunning and has many names: the devil, Lucifer, Beelzebub, antichrist, fallen angel, the great deceiver, great dragon, prince of darkness, son of perdition, the serpent, etc. Some newer names that can be added to him are the deviant one, the great disturber, and the confounder. Satan works upon our thoughts, and when we leave our guard down he can manipulate us, as if we were marionettes; he pulls all the strings. He is the one who says in our minds just go ahead and steal it, no one will care; go ahead and rape her, she wants it anyways; just shoot the gun and kill him; just lie, nobody will ever know the truth; make the company profits look better and fix the books, it is for the good of everybody; cheat on your spouse, they'll never know that you did; go ahead and rob that store, they have more than they need; go ahead and steal that credit card and buy whatever you want, the credit card company will have to pay for it; show everyone how strong you are and beat up the little creep, the runt should have been born bigger anyway; etc. These are only a few ways Satan persuades humanity, and he never ever, ever stops. Satan does not sleep, he has nothing but time to find ways to deceive and lead us astray. Recently, he has been very successful in doing this task.

Not only can Satan and the demons can make us kill, steal, dance naked through the streets, curse God, and hate anyone who is different than us; he can also make us feel paranoid, doubtful, depressed, lonely, suicidal, helpless, worthless, etc. However, God gave us a free will, and we need to surrender it to Him and not to Satan. God sent us the Holy Spirit, who will tell us whether we are on the right path, or making a wrong choice. Recently though, Satan has made great strides in deceiving us, and this is why there are so many people in prison today. Even with the prisons full, there are many more people who should be there and although they have temporarily escaped punishment on Earth; this will not be the case in death.

Satan has no patience, no love, no compassion, and no heart. He is filled with selfishness, arrogance, vanity, jealousy and wants to acquire as much as possible. He imparts these attributes upon us so that we will follow him. We become selfish and self-centered desiring big houses, designer clothes, fancy cars, expensive jewelry, big salaries, pretty girls, or handsome guys. We become so infatuated with physical appearances that we don't care about personalities; we are guided by our lust for the human flesh. Many people are prideful just as Satan, and this will lead them to their destruction either on Earth, or in the afterlife.

Satan does not want us to do God's 'will', because if we do, we will enter into Heaven, a place that Satan can no longer be, he is now an outcast. Satan is arrogant and may be saying to himself, "How God could let these pitiful creatures that have no power and who can actually die, be allowed into Heaven and I not allowed there?" How dare him! I'll teach him! I will destroy these insignificant creatures and I will show Him how truly great

I am. I am the great Lucifer, I am powerful, I am like God, I will have those creatures worship me and I will corrupt them to do my bidding. Satan is filled with nothing but self-delusions and he wants us to follow him. Satan is obsessed with himself (I, I, and I) and many people on Earth who follow suit are only concerned with pleasing themselves and care little for others.

When Satan had the Pharisees, Sadducees and some Jewish citizens make false accusations against Jesus to incite his death; Satan fell right into God's trap. God had chosen His Son to be the sacrificial lamb; one who would freely give up His life, so that many people could receive eternal life. Had Satan realized that Jesus actually represented a way to Heaven for humanity; he would have left Him alone and allowed Jesus to live out His life unharmed. Because Satan is prideful, he wanted to get even with God by having His Son murdered. He tried to have Jesus killed three times.

The first time was shortly after Jesus had been born to Mary. Satan confounded King Herod by making him believe that Jesus wanted to be the king of Israel. This thought enraged Herod so much; that in order to prevent this from becoming a reality, he ordered all the infant males up to two-years-old to be killed in Bethlehem, (Matthew 2:16–18). However, he was unsuccessful in having Jesus killed because Joseph, Mary's husband, had a dream (Matthew 2:13–14) warning him of Herod's treachery, and was told to take Mary and Jesus to Egypt.

The second attempt on Jesus's life, John (8:53–59), happened after Jesus proclaimed to be the fulfillment of the Torah's reading; in other words, to be the Messiah. This concept filled the Jewish people with so much hatred towards Jesus, they attempted to stone Him, but He escaped.

Lastly, Satan corrupted the Pharisees minds to be so envious of Jesus's popularity that they conceived a plot to have Him murdered. They not only wanted Jesus killed, but to be beaten; scourged by the Roman soldiers; and rejected by the Jewish people. Satan wanted God to hear the people cry out "We don't want your Son; we want the murderer Barabbas to live instead". After the trial, Jesus was forced to carry a cross upon His scourged-back, and to suffer further humiliation by dying a criminal's death through the heinous method of crucifixion. Satan not only believed he had prevailed over Jesus, but that he also ridiculed and insulted God by having His Son endure so many sufferings.

God is omnipotent and omniscient; whereas, Satan is not. As previously indicated, Satan intends to destroy the entire human race, but God will not permit this from occurring, a remnant will be saved. Part of Gods' plan to save humanity began when He brought into the world a young girl, who was about 15-years-old, to be the mother of His Son. She is known as the Virgin Mary and gave birth to Jesus. In time, the Virgin Mary would also be given the task of combating Satan. She would defeat the once mighty Satan by just submitting her 'will' to God.

How could she defeat Satan by just submitting her 'will' to God? First of all, she trusted God from the beginning, as we should all do. When she was told by the archangel Gabriel that God had chosen her to be the mother of His Son, she replied, "*Let His will be done to me*". It must be remembered that in those days, a woman found to be pregnant without a husband could be stoned to death; so by saying yes to God, she was potentially allowing herself to be killed, but her faith in God was greater than her fear of death.

Her faith was analogous to Abraham's faith in God. God had asked Abraham to sacrifice his only son Isaac to Him, and when he was about to do it, an angel of the Lord stopped him (Genesis, Chapter 22). As a reward for Abraham's faith, God promised Abraham that he would be the **father of many nations**. In like manner, Mary has been rewarded for her faith; she raised and loved Jesus, and had to endure the hardship of seeing her Son die on the cross. For her reward, God has appointed Mary to be the **mother of all people on Earth** and to be the queen of angels. She sits at the right hand side of her Son Jesus in Heaven and intercedes for us on Earth by asking God to hold back His promised chastisements. She is also calling for all of us to convert and to live righteously before the coming of the last days. In addition, when we find ourselves sub coming to evil temptations; we can call out for her help, she will send the angels to aid us defeat the demons.

These are the reasons why God choose Mary and not John the Baptist, or an angel to call humanity back to Him. God has a great deal of respect for all mothers, and most especially for the mother of His Son. Almost every person can say that during the course of their life they had cried out to their mother in a time of need?

Mary is no different than any other mother who does something for their children; she too has been known to intervene to her Son on people's behalf. For instance, it was Mary who requested that Jesus do something for the wedding couple who ran out of wine at their wedding feast. In John (2:1–11), she told the servers, "*do whatever he tells you*". In response to his mother's request, He did something by miraculously converting the water into wine; by this means she helped the wedding couple on their festive day.

Like John the Baptist, who was given the special task to call people to convert and follow Jesus; Mary, because of her status in Heaven, has also been given this identical call to lead the lost sheep of our age back to her Son. She is interceding to her Son, to be allowed to come to Earth and help people towards conversion. By what means is she helping us?

She has been presenting herself to visionaries, of all nationalities, throughout the world during the twentieth century. She has been seen by more visionaries in the twentieth century than any other century. Why? She is given messages to them that if mankind doesn't convert, then God will send impending cataclysmic chastisements upon the earth. Her warnings are real and she is calling for humanity to "repent now" and follow her Son before it is too late. She has told the visionaries that this is not a joke, time is short and Jesus is about ready to return; as a result she wants us all to be saved before the judgment day arrives. She has promised to all people in the world that a sign will appear in the sky as proof of her being here on Earth. This sign will be permanent and visible, but once it appears in the sky, it will be too late for many. The time for this sign to appear is not far off.

Chapter 3

A Time for Reaping

With God, there is no such thing as accidental. Everything is planned, and there is perfection in his plans. For instance; it was Adam and Eve who let out all the evils in the world when they disobeyed God and ate the fruit from the Tree of Life. However, it was Mary and Jesus who enabled mankind to be free from sin. It is much like what the Chinese call the Yin and Yang, where two separate energies form a perfect circle, God will take what appears to be two different events, and He will bring them together to form one unified event; in other words, symmetry.

Looking at this concept of symmetry and completeness, when Mary was pregnant with Jesus, *her body protected him* and *her blood fed him* the nutrients of life through her umbilical cord during the gestation period. At the moment she gave birth, her *water* broke and *blood* was issued during the birthing process and Jesus was born into our world. Jesus's life as a fetus was over, and He had now become an infant in our world.

Here is the symmetry of God's design, Christians are taught that Jesus's *body protects us* and His *blood feeds us* the nutrients required for spiritually life. When Jesus was speared upon the cross; *blood and water* issued from the wound, much like the water and blood issued from a woman during birthing. At that moment, His spirit left his body and entered into Heaven. In some respects, it was as if He was born as a new being in Heaven and by the means of His death, He plans to guide mankind there too. The completeness in God's plan becomes; in one episode, it is a woman who gives birth to mankind's life on Earth, but in the other episode, it is a man (Jesus) giving eternal life for mankind in Heaven.

For with God, there is always methodology to his designs, and the world will not come to an end at a random date, but instead at a time that completes fulfillment. The countdown for the end of the world actually started a long time ago in the Kingdom of Heaven. The battle between good and evil began an unknown number of years ago, when Satan stood by the side of God in Heaven. Satan's envy of God caused him and one-third of the holy angels to form an insurgency against God. However, Michael the archangel of God, along with the remaining two-thirds of God's holy angels, cast Satan and the other rebellious angels out of paradise. This revolt by Satan left a vacancy in Heaven, and with God there is no such thing as incompleteness. This void needs to be filled, but with whom or what? Did God created mankind to fill this vacancy with human souls?

If so, hypothetically the number of souls entering Heaven would equal the number of the angels (one-third) that revolted against God. The numbers could be in the billions or trillions of souls. Since the beginning of time there has been an estimated of 70-106 billion people who have lived. So, if God was going to fill Heaven only with souls equating to the number of fallen angels, it could be as few as 23-35 billion (one-third), of all the human beings that have ever lived.

The absolute number of souls reaching Heaven is unknown, but to God. However, there are biblical references indicating that more souls going may be going into Hell than Heaven. In the Book of Zechariah (13:8–9), it was written *"…two-thirds in it shall be cut off and die, but one-third shall be left in it.*" Another indication to the number of souls going to Heaven can be found in the parable about the wedding feast, Matthew (22:1–14). In this parable, the king orders his servants to go out and invite everyone they can to fill the banquet with guest for the wedding feast. They did as the king ordered, but it was found that one guest was not dressed appropriately for the occasion. The king had him bound and thrown out. The last line of the parable is *"Many are invited, but few are chosen."* This is direct reference towards humanity, in that many are invited to be in God's kingdom, but few are chosen.

Likewise, in Matthew (7:13–14), Jesus said, *"Enter through the narrow gate; for the gate is wide and the road broad that leads to destruction, and those who enter it are many. How narrow and constricted the road that leads to life. And those who find it are few."* If 50% of the people made it into Heaven, why wouldn't have Jesus have said something like "...narrow ...and... broad ... leads to life and **half** make it"? If 75% of the people made it into Heaven perhaps he would have said, "...narrow ... and... broad ... leads to life and **most** make it". He didn't say either of these statements rather he said, "**Few** make it". Jesus knows that many, many people deny the Holy Spirit, and they fall into Satan's traps because they won't heed to God's warnings.

Why is it so difficult to enter into Heaven? In order to be proven worthy to be citizens of Heaven, mankind must be first tempted by Satan and the fallen angels. We are not to side with them, but instead to remain devoted to God. God wants us to be devoted to our spouse, in doing so; we are proving to be faithful to God. God wants us to share the wealth He has given to us, and to help those of need; by responding as such, it shows of our compassion for the less fortunate. God wants us to use power and authority to guide humanity, but not to misuse it for personal gain. God wants us to forgive others and not seek revenge, by doing this we too will be pardoned for our sins.

It's apparent that a lot of souls are required to fill the void in Heaven, but possibly twice as many souls may fall into Hell. Does this sound fair? How could such a loving God send so many souls to Hell? He doesn't, and He doesn't want to see us go there, we choose to go into Hell by our choices in life.

Satan caused his demise when he opposed God, and it wasn't God who suddenly got mad at him one day and said, "Get out of here; I'm tired of seeing you." There is an expression that says, "Burn me once, shame of you, burn me twice, shame on me", which in essence God wants to prevent the "shame on me". In order to avoid this, God permits Satan to tempt us with power, greed, money, glory, fame and for material things that are upon the Earth. Those who reject these temptations will be the true souls proved worthy enough to be called the children of God. For they have already rejected Satan on Earth; they endured all hardships and showed loyalty, faith and love to God. We make this choice on Earth, and it is not God who arbitrarily says, "You're in, or you're out". We and we alone make this decision, by our actions made during our lifetime.

The end of our world as we know it could be at the time when the numbers of human souls have nearly filled this empty void, left by the demons. This being the case, Satan would be actively seeking to collect as many souls as possible before his time is up. The last of the souls that would enter into Heaven and conversely the last to fall into Hell will therefore come out of the great tribulation. The tribulation, which although is a time of great destruction and sorrow for humanity, caused by our disobedience and rebelliousness, is a beautiful opportunity given by God, as a last minute reprieve for human beings to convert. This is the absolute last time we will either choose for God or Satan, and those who select God, Heaven will be their eternal home; but for those who don't; Hell will be their home for eternity.

From the Book of Revelation (7: 9–17), "*I had a vision of a great multitude of people from every race, nation and tongue...wearing white robes...then one of the elders said to me, "who are these wearing white robes..." He said to me, these are the ones who survived the great distress (tribulation); they have washed their robes and made them white in the blood of the lamb.*"

If all of this did transpired as depicted; such that one-third of all human souls go to Heaven while two-thirds fall into damnation, then Heaven would be composed of one-third human souls with two-thirds of God's holy angels while Hell would consist of two-thirds human souls with one-third demonic angels. As can be seen, these numbers are comparable to one another with them both adding up to unity for both good and evil. In summary; God will have His kingdom of good, consisting of human souls and angels; whereas, Satan will have his kingdom of evil, consisting of lost human souls and demonic angels.

But what about the devil's as number being 666? The New Testament specifies the Son of Perdition will have the number 666. What could this number represent? Could it be a time in human history when two-thirds (2/3= 0.666) of humanity will have lost faith in God and rebelled against him, as did Satan and the fallen angels? Is it a secret societies code for the ultimate individual 'antichrist' that will do Satan's bidding of subjugating and pacifying humanity? Does it represent the last 'damned soul' that enters into Hell after the tribulation and completes the two-thirds of lost souls? Is it a time when two-thirds of the world has become evil and are being led by the antichrist? No one knows for sure.

When did this counting of souls begin, and will the twenty-first century be the time when the number of souls entering Heaven be completed? If this century brings on the tribulation, then what makes this time so unique? Many things have unfolded during the previous century, making it the most unequaled century ever. First of all, technological changes have made it possible for Satan to reprogram all of humanity. He can now easily reach out and teach his ways to all human beings on Earth via TV, Internet, movies, satellite dishes, cell phones, etc.

Furthermore, the twentieth century was unique for the Jews because of the re-establishment of Israel. In the Book of Revelation, the Jewish people are in Israel surrounded by their enemies. Prior to 1948, the Jewish people were scattered throughout the world and it wasn't until November 29, 1947 when the U.N. General Assembly declared a state for Israel. The enemies of Israel are still there with Syria, Egypt, Iran, Jordan and Iraq. There is still a great hatred by these countries towards the Jews and some of them have openly declared that Israel will be obliterated.

God had promised the Jewish people that they would have the 'promised land' at the end of time. However, there was a period in the Jewish timeline (starting at 597 B.C.E.) when the Jews were exiled, by Nebuchadnezzar II, for approximately seventy years. The exiled ended after 532 B.C.E., but it wasn't until ~520 B.C.E. that most of the Jews returned under Zerubbabel, and the foundations of the second Temple were laid. If those lost 70 years are added to the year 1947, the year Israel was declared a state by the U.N., the end of time may be in 2017. As previously mentioned, this coincides with both Pope Leo XIII prophecy of Satan's being given 100 years to test humanity and the Virgin Mary's first appearance at Fatima in 1917. When those 100 years given to Satan are added to 1917, the end of time calculates to be around the year 2017.

Another unique aspect that occurred in the twentieth century was the Blessed Virgin Mary's visitation to three young children at Fatima. She had given them messages that God was about ready to send impending chastisements upon the world. She implored for them to have the bishops of the world to consecrate Russia to her immaculate heart. It appears that Russia is going to be the instigator for the end times to take place; however, the bishops didn't heed her request.

Why were there three children and not one or two? What is the significance about the number three? Three is about one-third of the way to ten and it may represent the number of human beings who will still be living righteous life's at the second coming of Jesus. One-third could also represent the percentage of souls that will make it through the tribulation and enter into Heaven. As mentioned earlier, it could also be the percentage number, one-third; of all human beings who ever lived that will make it into Heaven.

The month of May appears to have some significant meaning for the end time. Is it coincidence Israel became a state on May 14, 1948 and the Virgin Mary first appeared in Fatima on May 13, 1917? Does the month of May represent a pivotal time in mankind's history? May is usually the period for farmers to sow seed; maybe it is being used as a symbolic time by Mary to sow in our hearts a new found love (conversion) for God before the time of harvest. Perhaps it represents a new season for the people of Israel, who are required to be present at the harvest time, to see their Messiah come in his Glory, as a conqueror of all that is unjust.

Another possibility for Mary's appearance in May can be explained by one of the Medjugorje visionaries, who said that God would place a permanent sign in the sky, which will be seen throughout the world, as affirmation of her presence upon Earth. Before this sign would appear, the visionaries would tell the priest of their choosing and in response he would fast for seven days. Afterwards, he is to inform the world ten days prior to the unfolding of this event.

The day of the week when this sign appears would be on a Tuesday, Wednesday or Thursday, between the months of March thru May, and would be on a little known saint's day; one that had great devotion to the Eucharist. One potential candidate is Saint Pascal, who was renowned for his devotion to the Eucharist, and his saint day is on May 17. Is it happenstance that the Virgin Mary first appeared at Fatima in **May** 1917 and in the year **2017**, May **17** is on a Wednesday, which coincides with one of the days of week given by the visionaries for this heavenly sign? It was also said that for those who had not converted before this sign, it would be too late for them.

Why did the Blessed Virgin Mary come to Medjugorje, the second most important apparition site in all of history, in 1981? She told the Medjugorje visionaries that after her visit there, it would be the last time she would appear on Earth. If she is not going to appear on Earth any longer, it means that Satan is defeated, and if he is defeated, it means the end of the world as we know it. What if the year 1981, was not just a random year? For instance, what if the year 1981was combined with something of meaning; such as, the number of years her Son lived in this world?

Jesus may have been born about 6B.C, two years before the death of King Herod in 4B.C. However, there remains a degree of uncertainty, in the exact date of Jesus's crucifixion, which has been estimated to be anywhere from 26A.D. to 33A.D. Many scholars believe that he was crucified in 30A.D. while others ascertain that it was on 31A.D. Assuming Jesus was born 6B.C. and crucified in 30A.D; then he would have been 36 years old when he died. Adding 36 years to the year1981, calculates to be the year 2017. Jesus had been on Earth for 36 years and perhaps God gave his mother, our Holy Mother, the same amount of time for her most instructive and comprehensive messages, at Medjugorje, for humanity to convert and return us to Him before the world comes to an end.

There is no exact way in determining the end of time, but is it pure chance that the year 2017 keeps coming up? Yes, one can always find ways to force numbers to fit the logic that one desires, but in reality it is God time table and it is set up to follow a path of logical order, and not in a haphazard manner. If the year 2017 is close to his timeframe, then what would have aroused God to have so much anger to want to destroy the world? What changed in humanity to cause this?

Chapter 4

An Era of Change

A reference to the end times comes from the Apostle Paul, in his Second Letter to Timothy (3:1–9) he defines the conditions of humanity during those last days. He writes that people will be callous, self-centered, lovers of self, lovers of wealth, proud, arrogant, ungrateful, irreligious, slanderous, licentious (morally and sexually unrestrained and disregarding rules), brutal, traitors, hating good, reckless, conceited, lovers of pleasure rather than God, disobedient to parents, and that spouses will be unfaithful to one another.

If Satan wanted to destroy the church, what steps would he take? Given that at the turn of the twentieth century, most individuals were God-fearing people; he would have people question the laws of God, just as he did before his fall. How does one make people question God's laws? As mentioned, one way is to have people to stop being dependent on Him, as they did in the past when they would pray for rain so that their crops could grow, pray for the health of a sick person, pray to endure hardships, pray when natural disasters happened, or pray because they felt God would punish them if they didn't.

Just as Satan convinced Adam and Eve to eat the fruit from the Tree of Knowledge, so that their eyes would be opened and they would be like God; Satan wants us to open our eyes to our new found technology. In accepting these advances in knowledge, we may fall under the misbelief that prayer is unnecessary.

Once we understand weather patterns, we won't need to pray to God; once we comprehend how to heal the human body, we won't need to pray to God; once we learn to explore the skies, the seas and recognize natures' ways, we won't need to pray to God; once we live in luxury, we won't need to pray to God for basic necessities. We will have secured hidden knowledge, and understand on how the world and universe operates. Once we have accomplished this, we will believe God never really existed and be deluded that we are control of our destiny. We will assume that we can conduct our lives just as Paul depicted in his Second Letter to Timothy.

Yes– this is the strategy of Satan; it is one of a slow change that would wean us off our dependency upon God. A change so slight, we wouldn't believe anything was any different than it was previously. However, as each year passes the effect would eventually become greater and greater until the reference point of godliness and righteousness are no longer recognizable.

There were an abundant number of changes for humanity during twentieth century, many of them began during WWI and continued afterwards. The first part of the twentieth century was considered the Victorian age. It was a time of mutual respect between people; it was a time when God was worshipped and Sundays were a day of rest. It was an innocent time, but before long, in the second decade of the twentieth century, the world would be at war. When this war was over, arising from the ashes of destruction; change would begin, and a new type of men and women would emerge.

Women have always been the cornerstone in the household. They did the duties that men did not want to do; women were humble, and in actuality they were the glue that bound the family together. They raised the children, washed them, fed them and made sure that did their homework and chores before they put them off to bed. It was women, and not men, who insured the stability of the house, but they were rarely given the respect they deserved and often were taken advantage of, and even ridiculed by their husbands. Therefore they struggled for emancipation for not only political freedom, but they sought to be relived from the confinement of their duties as housewives. They sought careers and greater freedom from their traditional role as mothers, and soon after World War I, they would be granted their desires. This erosion of the women's role as the head of the household would tragically lead the nation; hence the world, into constant downward spiraling abyss throughout the twentieth century, as it will be described in the subsequent decades.

1920s

What better time for Satan to begin his crusade to destroy mankind's morality than the in Roaring 20's. World War I had just ended a few years prior, and there was jubilation throughout the world. Industry was humming and Wall Street was now mankind's new god. This was a time of unprecedented material wealth, and there were wholesale changes in prior taboos. Women, so-called flappers, were now entering into bars, which historically only men would go in to. The only exception of women who would be in bars prior to that time, were the ladies of the evening. This was Satan's strategy, with women now drinking, there began a loosening of their moral values. Soon, they would now find themselves being counted as one of the promiscuous women, who were once being outcast by society and were now giving birth to unwanted children.

However for these women a savior of a different calling came to their rescue. Margaret Sanger, a nurse, who in the year 1917 set up the first birth control clinic in The United States. She must have been elated having these now loose women coming to her for ways to prevent conception. Although not all women that visited bars lost their virtue, it was only the beginning of the onslaught, and as time would continue, the slide of women's moral values would be so numerous, the word virgin would be almost unheard of.

Along with the changes in women in the 1920s, there came a time of lawlessness. Women had been advocates of prohibition of liquor for many years, and in1919 they were victorious in pushing through the Eighteenth Amendment of the United States Constitution. It established 'Prohibition' in the United States; however, it did allow a time delay before it would fully take effect; only after each state's ratification, which was completed in the year 1922.

These good intentioned women unwittingly provided Satan with fresh ammunition to seduce souls. As it turned out, this new bill brought about a whole new wave of criminal activity and criminals. These men were organized and took crime to an all new level. They were called gangsters and they murdered on the streets, blackmailed, bribed public officials to get their personal interest done, manipulated elections, initiated the sale of illegal alcohol, and as time progressed they would sell illegal drugs. They would give themselves the name 'Mafia' and many unions and construction businesses were under their control. In time, out in the desert of Nevada, these men would build their houses of prostitution and gambling, in order to extract every penny they could from people. This city would be called sin city, whose motto would be "What happens in Vegas stays in Vegas". All of these things in reality were being manipulated by Satan, so that he could seduce souls; namely, for us to overly indulge in the pleasures of this world.

1930s

The 1930s were a time of economic depression, a mini-chastisement by God, and the world suffered from their desire of longing for material wealth. People suffered loss of farms, homes, livelihoods, and families fell apart. The good old days were over and now Satan was wreaking havoc in everyone's lives. Soon, he was setting up the world for a devastating war. The greed of Wall Street brokers caused a worldwide depression that sent millions of people into poverty. It was a desperate time; especially in Germany, where the people were already suffering by having to pay reparations for WWI. The German debt, set by the Inter-Allied Reparations Commission in 1921, was to be 100,000 tons of gold (the sum in today's dollars of $4.5 trillion dollars), which turned out to be an insurmountable amount of money to be paid back by the German people. It destabilized the German economy and politics so much so, that this too fell into Satan's strategy. It would be one that would eventually cause the destruction for most of the world.

This debt handed down by the Inter-Allied Reparations Commission caused the dissatisfaction of the German people with their political leaders and in the 1930s it resulted in a change of German leadership. An evil man named Adolph Hitler was nothing more than a private in the German army in WWI; however, by the year 1934 he would be Chancellor of Germany. Adolph was a vindictive man, who hated the conditions of the Treaty of Versailles, and he would build up the German economy and army within a short period of six years. This evil man would plunge the world into another world war (predicted by the Virgin Mary at Fatima) far greater than WWI, and it would forever change all of humanity. Satan was methodically manipulating humanity to do his bidding and this was only the beginning.

1940s

The 1940s began as a time of crisis. World War II had already started on September 1, 1939, Germany invaded Poland with subsequent declarations of war on Germany, by France and most of the countries of the British Empire and Commonwealth. By the 1940s, WWII was like a ravaging fire destroying everything it came in contact with, part of the devastation resulted in over seventy million human lives being sacrificed. It also accounted for more than six million Jews being victims of national persecution by the Nazis. Satan's plan to exterminate the Jews had almost become a reality. For if there were no Jews; Satan wins and God loses.

In addition there were so many men fighting during World War II, that women were needed to fill the factories to make the war machines. With their husbands gone to war; many of these women began affairs with other men and soon a common letter received by soldiers would start as "Dear John, I have found someone else…"

The effect of this war upon women would be even greater than expected. As time went on, more and more women would be in the working world. Now they were making money and feeling a sense of independence from men. They no longer needed men, and they didn't want to stay at home raising children; they wanted to be like men, to carouse and have fun.

The downfall of the typical family had begun with the beginning of WWII. Divorces, infidelity and promiscuity were on the rise, and correspondingly there were fewer mothers at home guiding their children; instead these working women were either too tired to spend the time needed for child rearing, or they were spending time with men. Indeed, Satan's handiwork was proving to be successful. The erosion of the American family values was now on its way.

This war likewise brought upon our culture a new generation of weapons with properties capable of mass destruction. This weapon, called an A-bomb, was capable of incinerating human flesh within seconds, and if it fell into the wrong hands; it could possibly destroy all of humanity. Two of these bombs, with a combine explosive power equal to 33 thousand tons of TNT, killed a quarter million people when they were dropped on the Japanese cities of Hiroshima and Nagasaki during WWII.

As WWII continued, a backwards peasant country began to manufacture weapons and eventually they beat Hitler's mighty army, all the way back to Germany. This backwards country was known as Russia; recounting the words of the Virgin Mary *"If Russia is not consecrated to my immaculate heart, Russia would spread her evil ways throughout the world"* was coming true. Russia had now arrived as a power, all as a result of World War II, and after the war it would gather in satellite states to become known as the USSR. The USSR was the epitome of satanic belief, in which a set of countries forbade the worship of God and in many cases murdered thousands of priest and destroyed churches.

When WWII ended, numerous individuals including Klaus Fuchs and Morris Cohen sold the secrets for making atomic bombs to the Soviet Union and they were responsible for this atheistic country becoming a super power. In the 1950s fusion bombs, known as H-bombs, were developed with one of them having the explosive power equal to 25 million tons of TNT. Both the Soviet and United States militaries built up nuclear arsenals consisting of tens of thousands of these H-bombs. There was now enough atomic power to rip the Earth apart. It was the beginning of the cold war. It was a time where paranoia would reach into the homes of every American family. Communism would be a hated word and many Americans would say, "The only good commie is a dead commie". It was a philosophy that would cause more innocent lives to be shortened.

As can be seen, Satan now has the ability to destroy the human race in a single day, and all he has to do to accomplish this is to provoke any nuclear country into a confrontation. This event which did not happen in the twentieth century is still a real threat for humanity and as tensions rise in the world, and they will, this type of war may still occur.

1950s

The 1950s was a time when the world was rebuilding itself from the devastation and destruction of WWII. At that time, the world was at relative peace except for a war known as the Korean War. The North Koreans were a communistic country, along with China and the USSR. This little country was involved in a war with a contingent of soldiers, from NATO countries, who were there to prevent communism from taking over the southern province of the peninsula. It was the USSR spreading its' errors into neighboring countries, which resulted in eight hundred thousand people being killed.

It was a time when people had become war weary, but also a period when they were very leery of a total communistic takeover of the world. School children were taught to duck under their desks in the event of a nuclear war, and at the same time it was still a period of innocence. It was an era of American pride, which believed that nobody could defeat the powerful United States. It would be a belief that would lead America down a perilous path filled with arrogance, which would bring about future wars.

America was enjoying an unprecedented time of prosperity. Most States had 'Blue laws' that prohibited selling goods on Sundays, and families would spend time together either visiting other family members, or doing an activity; such as, going to the amusement park, beach, or maybe even going to see a ballgame. There would be plenty of barbecues, and families would relax before going to work the following Monday. Before too long, however, with Satan urging us on to accumulate more wealth, stores would now be opened on God's day of rest, and there would be many other whole-sale changes in our society, still to come.

The 1950s were a time when children would go to school, and begin the day by saying the pledge of allegiance with the words "One Nation under God", along with the Lords' Prayer; that was the case a least until the year 1963. It was in 1963, when the United States Supreme Court ruled in favor of an American atheist named Madalyn Murray O'Hair, founder of the organization of American

Atheists. She was its president from the year 1963 and she wanted all religious prayer banned in public schools. It was at this point the United States began to break away from being a righteous nation, by delineating God from our nation's existence.

This although not the precedence for the 'the end of the world' was however crucial to the overt antichristian world that we live in today. How long would it take for children to say to themselves; if we can't say God's name in school, then He must be bad? It was a clear victory for Satan, when the United States Supreme Court did his bidding and ruled by an 8:1 decision in favor of an atheist. In less than fifty years Satan had reduced sentiment towards God, by eliminating prayer in public places, and he wasn't finished yet.

1960s

The late 1960s experienced further breakdown of the family as a unit. Another war loamed over the country, and soldiers were sent to Vietnam to once more fight communism. The Vietnam War cost the United States 58,000 lives and 350,000 wounded soldiers. It also resulted between one and two million Vietnamese deaths. The Vietnam War was much more devastating than deaths, causalities, or economic cost. It revamped the perception of the American people, who thought the U.S. government did what was in the best interest for its citizens. Tens of thousands of young men's lives were shortened, caused by a philosophy and egotism of those who were elected into office.

This war turned the youth of America against the government and they began anti-establishment groups called 'hippies'. They began partaking in free sex, drugs, living in communes, and having atheistic practices. Other youths even indulged in satanic practices by partaking in multi-partner fornication for their new master; Satan. They no longer believed in a benevolent God who watched over them day and night; rather, it was do whatever you wanted to do, because life is short. A new age of children were being born, a generation filled with *rebelliousness, immorality, lust, and greed.* These practices by these children would eventually be followed by each successive generation, with each one pushing 'the envelope open' more and more.

The 1960s and 70s brought upon a way of new wave of music that expounded the imagination of young couples having sex in a car with the wiper blades orchestrating their rhythmic activity, or a woman wondering if her lover will respect her in the morning and whether they were creating a love child. Sex had become open and was promoted by clothing designers, television, XXX pornographic movies and Penthouse magazine. It was the pride in these women that enticed them to show off their bodies, and as written in Malachi (3:19) *"For lo, the day is coming, blazing like an oven, when all the proud and evildoers will be stubble. And the day that is coming will set them on fire…"* If these audacious displays by women, who were showing off their anatomy, weren't bad enough to anger God; then those individuals, who openly worshipped Satan would soon come on the scene and arouse His wrath.

In the late 1960s, a diabolical man named Anton Szandor LaVey founded the Church of Satan. This was the first organized church in modern times, propagating satanic religious philosophy as the symbol of personal freedom and individualism. LaVey declared the founding of the Church of Satan, and renumbered the year 1966 as the year 'one' for the first year of the age of Satan. Some notable members included Jayne Mansfield, Sammy Davis Jr., and Marilyn Manson. LaVey was inviting Satan into his life, and was seducing even the affluent to join him to worship Satan. He even wrote the 'Satanic Bible' and 'The Book of Lucifer'. Satan was now being invited into the souls of the foolish by their own request.

Not only was Satan's plan for creating a world consumed with rebelliousness coming into fruition in the 1960s, but the age of knowledge with great medical achievements were emerging; subsequently, it was the beginning of the time where mankind felt an independence from God. By 1967, a doctor named Christian Barnard performed the first human heart transplant. Although the patient, Louis Washansky died soon after; it was the opening of Pandora's Box. Soon surgeons would be performing transplants of all sorts, and the need for miracle healings would no longer be needed, mankind could now equate to being like God. No longer would it be 'it was God's will' that they died. Just as Joel prophesized (Joel 3:1-2) *"in the end times knowledge will be poured out on mankind."* This was just the beginning of the pouring out of knowledge; for in the decades following, more and more inventions were derived, with some of them even astounding mankind.

1970s

As each decade progressed, Satan and his demons were moving forward with their objective of instilling absolute bedlam upon society. The country was still bogged down in a war in Vietnam, and students were protesting throughout the country, some of which turned violent. The government would send troops to these demonstrations, and at the Kent State University campus, the National Guard would open fire on the students killing four and wounding nine. In the 1970s Chicago demonstrations, Richard Daley, the Mayor of Chicago sent out the police force, who brutally beat the demonstrators with night sticks, all of this being done in the 'land of the free'. The youth were revolting against the government and chaos followed chaos.

The 1970s was a time when Hollywood started to teach a whole generation of youth about disobedience, lack of respect for authority, and to follow immoral behavior; such as that depicted in the movie "Animal House". Not only were the youth not listening to their government, they became a disobedient lot towards their parents.

The 1970s also launched a new wave of electronic developments, with two innovations that would forever change humanity for better and worse. These worldwide altering inventions were the cellular phone and personal computer, and in time they would alter the way we would communicate with one another. These devices would in essence reduce the quality time that people previously had spent with one another. Families would not socialize as much; instead family members were glued to the computer and/or devote enormous amount of time on the cell phone networking with their friends.

Several decades later, in the 1990s, another means of communicating with others was conceived and it required the use of a personal computer. It was called the Internet, and it would contain volumes of information readily accessible to anyone who owned a computer and connected to this 'Web'. It would create a social center called 'Facebook', offer dating sites, and make things easily accessible that were previously difficult to come by; such as buying guns, methods on how to make bombs, viewing of pornography, and the ability to access personal financial accounts and secret government files. Although great volumes of knowledge could be retrieved on the Internet, it could easily be misused by corrupt minded people to negatively impact our lifestyles, and now the whole world was being seduced, including those individuals in the poorest of nations.

1980s

Music got louder, bolder and more vulgar as time went on. Soon we were hearing a constant barrage of the "f word" in rap music. Satan was using music to propagate his vulgar attitudes, teaching children to become more rebellious and disobedient to their parents. They began to experiment with sex at a younger age, and the number of teenage pregnancies increased. Hollywood was teaching youth about sex though movies like 'Risky Business', 'Bachelor Party' and disrespect for their parents' property in quaint movies like 'Sixteen Candles'. It was hard to find a television show that didn't make the man of the house look like an idiot, rather than a respected parent. Hollywood scripts went out of their way to have the wife ridicule their spouse, or the children belittling their father. It was a time when there was little respect for anyone that had authority, just as Satan envisioned it would be.

The youth in the 1980s were called the "Me Generation" and were focused only upon themselves; their image, their money, their clothes, and their looks. The stock market, commonly referred to as Wall Street, was worshipped by the masses, and soon corporations were bowing down to the edicts of stockbrokers, who were demanding that corporate America grow 10% a year. With corporate America being the pawns of Wall Street, these stockbrokers would be rewarded with huge bonuses, Rolex watches and luxury cars. However, brokers would severely punish any company if it didn't grow by 10% a year. This was accomplished by selling large quantities of stock for any underperforming company; thereby causing their share value to drop. So, in order to appease their newly found god, corporate America began to downsize their work force to make their financial earnings look better, despite the fact thousands of lives were being devastated.

This worked for a while, but Wall Street kept on yelling more, we want more growth. So in response to their god, corporate America got a better idea; they would move their factories outside the country to places like Mexico and Canada, both having a cheaper labor force. It worked at first, but Wall Street soon grew discontented with corporate earnings, and more sacrifices were needed to quench their thirst for money.

Corporations went to the jugular by sending jobs and parts of their companies to China, which is one of the countries with highest rating concerning atheistic practices. Corporate America was now lying in bed with Satan, causing more misery and tragedies for the Christian workers in the free world. Once more, both unscrupulous corporate CEOs and presidents were raking in the big bonuses and so were 'the boys' on Wall Street. Their satisfaction quickly waned and before too long and with an unquenchable thirst for wealth, corporate America found that they could buy off our "supposedly trusted" elected congressional members of congress. By filling the pockets of these dishonest elected officials with money; they would have them remove any tariffs, or taxes on their products coming from abroad, most especially from China. This removal of taxes and tariffs was called the North American Free Trade Agreement (NAFTA). Over time this resulted in the government collecting fewer and fewer tax dollars from American workers pay checks.

Although not apparent at the moment, this alteration in the philosophy of corporations will eventually bring forth the events foretold in the Book of Revelation (18:2–3) *"… fallen, fallen, is Babylon the great. She is a cage for every unclean spirit and all nations have drunk the wine of her licentious passion … and the merchants of the Earth grew rich from her drive to luxury."*

1990s

The 1990s brought upon the world even more lust for money, and a new generation of teenagers called 'gamers'. They would play games like 'Dungeons and Dragons' throughout the night and their minds no longer be focused on education, instead they would become polluted with satanic influences. They became lazy and expected to be waited on hand and foot by loving parents. These indolent individuals put aside the basic lesson on how to get into Heaven. It was a simple message that Jesus taught his disciples at the time when He washed their feet. He told them that if He being the master was cleaning their feet, then likewise they must serve others to be considered the children God. Satan once more found a way to corrupt the hearts of many individuals, and it was by having individuals being callous about the needs of others.

More satanic seductions started when girls began to be influenced by singers like Madonna, who was renowned for her erotic on-stage performances. In many instances, cities had to have police present during her performance to ensure that she didn't violate any of the cities' decency codes. Young girls were emulating her, along with other rock musicians who were equally depraved. The youth were revolting more and more; their gods were video games, drugs, sex, alcohol, and they maintained a total disregard for anyone older.

School policies were also being modified to fit the new norm. Instead of school books being passed out in sex education classes; they were passing out condoms. It was like a rubber stamp telling the youth that it was all right to commit fornication, as long as you use a condom. Satan knew that he was becoming more successful in brainwashing our youth. You can imagine seeing him, rubbing his hands together with a malicious smile upon his face and saying, "fornication, I want to see more fornication".

In 1991, a new war in the Middle East was erupting. An evil dictator named Saddam Hussein invaded a neighboring country, thereby getting NATO involved. The war was short lived, with a NATO victory eradicating Saddam's troops from Kuwait. However, in the year 2003 another Iraqi war with NATO began and Saddam was toppled from this Muslin country. Approximately at the same timeframe, another evil man named Osama Bin Laden would direct a terrorist attack against the United States of America, and a whole new type of war would begin. This war was called by President George W. Bush "A War on Terrorism". Osama Bin Laden had been hiding in Afghanistan, a Muslin country ruled by the Taliban; a group of religious fanatics who hate all Christians, Jews, western culture and believed in the subjugation women. In essence, they put themselves on par with God and felt they had the right to kill anyone with differing beliefs or ideologies. When they refused to give up Osama Bin Laden for trial, NATO was once more at war. Throughout this war, supposed Islamic clerics were encouraging women and children to be suicide bombers and to kill as many westerners as possible. Their cry was kill, kill, kill. It appeared as if Satan was setting up the world for a Muslin-Christian War, and as time continued into the next millennium, more and more Muslims would buy into the Taliban beliefs.

A major event happened in the 1990s when the Soviet Union collapsed. It appeared that the Virgin Mary's Fatima warning about Russia was uncalled for. Interestingly, after the breakup of the USSR, the Russians needed financial support from the west and they received it, avarice investors saw it as a large propensity for an economic gain. In reality though, Russian still remained at odds with America and in the succeeding decades into the new millennium, they would be using this "investment money" to manufacture weapons, which they would sell to every terrorist group in the world, including the extremist Muslims, most of whom were anti-American. Mary's warnings about Russia would remain as perilous as it did in 1917.

2000s

In the 2000s, Wall Street was still obsessed with money, and now the banks of the world joined them. Many unscrupulous mortgage companies and banks were falsifying individual's incomes, so they could qualify them for a loan. They would bundle these mortgages, and sell them to unwitting brokers. However, at the same time, the greedy commodity traders caused the price of oil to reach $146 per barrel; consequently, causing the price of fuel to double. Soon afterwards, many homeowners found that they could no longer afford to pay their mortgages because they were using the money to pay for fuel. The consequences of these actions were bad loan after bad loan failed due to greediness, resulting in many businesses to fold. Other companies would experience financial losses, as fewer people were buying their products.

Eventually the economy slowed so much that it caused many companies to cut their workforce. The whole world was now paying this heavy price of a recession/depression due to the insatiable need of Wall Street for money. Families were now suffering; some in which, both parents lost their jobs, and families were experiencing more arguments and innocent children were being affected by their quarrels.

There were more changes in society as well. Satan was still brain-conditioning young people through Hollywood. In the 1950s, programs on TV were "The Lucy Show" (in which Ricky and Lucy slept in different beds), "Leave it to Beaver" (a program about Mr. and Mrs. Cleaver raising their sons), "Father knows Best", "My Three Sons" (a show about widower raising three boys), etc. By the 2000s, Hollywood was influencing young women with programs; such as, "Girls Gone Wild", "Mean Girls", and "The Hottest Girl in America"; to name a few, all personified girls as being perverted, selfish, lustful, and licentious.

Other television programs showed more and more nudity, and there were vivid scenes added with couples being engaged in sexual activity. There was less TV censorship than there was in the early programming years. From this point in time and onwards, children not only learn sexual activity at an earlier age, but they began practicing it too, all due to the perverted minds of script writers.

An adult magazine called "Hustler" had become very graphic, which featured nude women in erotic positions, and California was over-flowing with places that made pornographic movies. Glamour magazines, drugs, peer pressure, radio talk shows, all of which were manipulating women to be sexy and/or sex objects. Satan had managed the degeneration and exploitation of women, and it was in full swing. More and more women were openly and proudly declaring themselves, as being lesbians. It was not much different as it was during the days of Sodom and Gomorrah, when homosexuality was at its peak and mankind defied the laws of nature, to satisfy their perverted lusts. No rules, no God to hold them back from doing their thing. As some free minded people would say, "Oh there is nothing wrong with it; they are just expressing themselves as individuals". The result of this free mindedness was a huge number of babies being born outside of marriage.

According to the National Center for Health Statistics, the number of unwed mothers in the United States rose significantly from 5% in the 1950s, to 40% by 2007, with almost one million teenagers each year becoming pregnant. At the same time, the number of single parents rose from 11% in the 1970s, to 31% by 1996. Some of these single parents were unwed mothers while others were the result of divorce. A study conducted by the University of Maryland listed the number of divorces per 1000 married women being 10% in the1950s, which rose to over 22% by the 1980s. The significance with this data, of both unwed mothers and divorced mothers, showed the instability and disintegration of the family unit was on the rise.

Mothers were at work and children ended-up being raised by a stranger, or they watched themselves. Proper guidance that should have been given to the kids by parents was not present. There was very little discipline in the household when these adolescents misbehaved, and if there was discipline; they had been taught by the school system to turn their parents into Child Protective Services. It is no surprise that these juveniles began getting into trouble and became ever so much more disobedient to their parent(s). It was a major victory step for Satan; namely, the destruction of family virtue while at the same time he was gaining significant influence over our youth, a lost generation of young people left without proper guidance or love.

Ultimately, this abandoned generation of adolescents, will allow Satan's campaign to come into full stride by them not wanting to attend church, thus denying God's presence in their lives. They remained as materialistic as their parents, who taught them that going to church occurred only on Christmas and Easter days. Instead of worshipping God, they opted to accept Santa Claus as the one they worship. One should wonder; where did religious aspects of Christmas go to? We no longer celebrate the birth of our Lord Jesus Christ. There was once a time when people would exchange gifts, as tokens of need rather than giving gifts of opulence, or upmanship. Over the years, Christmas has become a materialistic celebration with people worshipping presents, not Jesus. Ironically, instead of joy and happiness during Christmas time, many people became unhappy if they didn't get the most gifts, right gift or most expensive gift.

In today's world, the financial gains for retailers and, of course Wall Street, depend upon the sales at Christmas. By July, stores were already preparing for the Christmas shopping season. People became more worried about what they are going to buy or get for Christmas than going to church. Satan has accomplished to take over what was once a religious holiday, a time to celebrate the birth of our Lord Jesus Christ, and of our salvation, into one of materialism. Interestingly, if one rearranges the letters in Santa, it also spells Satan. Once more Satan has taken something good and made it into evil. One must always remember that Satan always tries to mimic God.

Other events of phasing out God in our lives started when corporate America changed from giving out Christmas bonuses to year-end bonuses. They no longer wanted to be affiliated with God. The world of business meant having factories in atheistic, Muslim, Hindu and Buddhist countries, and they didn't want to offend them, but they didn't care about offending those Christians, who made these companies profitable.

Terrorism in the 2000s was still on the rise, and the cost of these 'terroristic wars' was becoming massive. The beliefs of these fanatics were spreading, and the free countries had to expend more resources on counterterrorism. Additional security and devices were implemented by the governments of the world in order to track these men. Satellites made it possible to follow these wicked men's movements either from the sky, or by listening in on their cellular phone conversations. Additional resources were required to enable governments to discover terroristic plots, even as they were in the process of being realized. And by using supercomputers it was now possible to research on the Internet what these extremists were up to; i.e., methods to make bombs, purchases of explosive chemicals, biochemical warfare, etc. All of this technology being required to discover the intentions of these evil doers also meant a loss of freedoms for the civilized world. In time, these same tracking devices may be very well used by the anti-Christ, in order to maintain control and track those individuals deemed unacceptable "Christians".

2010s

The Catholic Church was reeling from the improper behavior of some of its priests and people were abandoning their faith.

Other Christian denominations were propagating homosexual and lesbian individuals to preside over their congregations. The judicial laws were encouraging the rights for gay couples to be married and furthermore the justice system was promoting the rights for euthanasia. The whole world abandoned God and flaunted their sinfulness in His face. They used the judicial system and overly free-minded individuals to promote and give blessings for their sinful desires, and they were granted them.

The world economic collapse that propagated in 2008 resulted with some countries approaching bankruptcy. The European monetary system, EURO, was under duress. Countries couldn't afford to pay their employees, and they wanted the tax payers to pay more taxes, which led to riots and instability. A great degree of hot-bloodedness cascaded into other countries; such as, Tunisia, Egypt, Syria, Yemen, Libya, and Jordan. Some of these countries were taken over by the military, while others were controlled by the rebels, or Islamic fundamentalists.

Egypt, which once had a security pact with Israel, negated this treaty after the military took over the government. Anti-Semitism and anti-Christianity was growing, and rogue nations like Iran wanted to acquire nuclear weaponry. They sought out help for their missile and nuclear program from non-other than Russian (like a ghost that haunt us, we keep on hearing the Virgin Mary's Fatima prediction about Russia). Iranian advancements in medium range ballistic missiles (MRBMs) succeeded, and they could fire a missile with enough range to reach Israel. The question is whether Israel will attack Iran before a nuclear missile is sent towards them.

The 2010s resulted in a world consumed by: economic stress, starvation, hatred spilling over between religions and countries, evil people acquiring the ability to destroy the world, and further abandonment of God. Satan's plan to slowly distance humanity from God was in full swing, and the stage for the colossal battle between Satan and God has now been set up. Satan has the means; he has gathered people to his side and created enough hate in the world to bring on this final war.

The past hundred years was an era of slow, but steadily dwindling changes in our society. Satan has altered the conditions in which we live in, and he has acquired a multitude of unwitting partners to do his bidding for the final battle. No wonder why the Virgin Mary came to Fatima in 1917. She wanted to warn us of Satan's manipulative powers and upon closer examination of these social transformations, it will be understood why humanity is currently on the precipice for its ultimate demise. We have been warned! It is going to happen! The world will end soon!

Chapter 5

A World Fallen Into Social Decay

As society unraveled throughout the twentieth century, it is impossible to record the total amount of chaos and decay that ensued as a result of mankind's wanton disregard for each other and nature itself, but it has been unmatched in history. Each day there are news reports of killings, thefts, dishonest public officials, economic collapse, political mayhem in all parts of the world, suicides, gay rights, weather extremes (record amounts of flooding, snow, heat, drought, along with storms, tornadoes and hurricanes), atrocities in the church, sexual crimes, sex scandals, white-collar crime, evil dictators, etc.

We can now see how evil is running amuck throughout the world, and this being the case, an alarm should be sounding off in our heads with the words *warning, warning*, you inhabitants of Earth. Many biblical writers refer to the end times, as a period of lawlessness that will bring on the Second Coming of Jesus; such as written in Matthew (24:13) *"Because of the increase of wickedness and lawlessness (evil-doing), the love of many will grow cold, but he who stands firm to the end will be saved."* Jesus pointed to a time of unruliness, and the love of many waning cold may be referring to those people who reject God. At the end of time, the number of these lawless individuals will become exceedingly large and since God is no longer in their lives, they tend to ignore the Ten Commandments, the very essence of the God's law.

Paul spoke of a time of anarchy in Thessalonians (2:7), although he was referring to the lawlessness that was already at work in his time, it can be inferred that this same resistance towards goodness would corrupt people, and then grow at an exponential rate until the cataclysmic end of humanity. Also, taken from Paul's letter to Timothy 2 (3:1–9), at the end times society will deteriorate so much; it will succumb to every immoral evil facet of life, and those times would be worse than the days of Sodom and Gomorrah.

As each generation of children is born, they learn behaviors from that time period. The children born in the 50s learned different values than those born in the 60s, 70s, etc... Each generation sequentially has moved further away from God, and as people stop worshipping Him, they no longer have a reference point between what is right and what is wrong. It would be as if we had strayed away from using zero as our starting reference point and instead began counting at forty. As time goes on, and we continually accept more deviations from the norm, the reference point gets farther away from the truth. Eventually it will become an 'anything goes' type society, living solely for pleasures. At first, society will not appear to be much different than it was in the past, and any current problems will be passed off as just minor divergences from the norm. Eventually, these complications will turn into an avalanche, and the whole world will be caught up in absolute chaos. This chaos is in itself the sign showing that humanity is following the path headed towards the great tribulation. As there is with any new beginning, a first step is required, and for the case of the human race, our downfall began by denying the existence of God.

Church attendance (the apostasy)

As the end times approach, there will be plagues both seen and unseen. The visible plagues will consists of viruses and diseases never heard of or seen before; while the unseen plagues will be a demonic infestation. These demons will lead people further away from righteousness, and there will be a great loss of faith in God (the great apostasy), as foretold in the bible. Even with humanities' disgrace, Heaven will make attempts to change the fundamental thinking of the inhabitants of Earth so that we could be led back to God's grace. Few people will respond to this calling, instead many will continue to follow the path of the devil.

Satan boasted to God that he was going to put an end to His church, once and for all time. If Satan could convince people from believing in a Supreme Being, he would establish this as his means to achieve victory. Satan brought upon the world, new concepts, and perceptions that have altered many individuals' theological belief in the existence of a deity. In the 1950s, 74% of all Catholics attended church on Sundays and within fifteen years, or near the end of the 1960s, this number dropped to 60% and by 2010 it was < 40%. That is almost a 46% drop in church attendance over a period of fifty years, just in the United States alone.

According to a '2009' Pew study, in the same timeframe, four American-born Catholics have left the church for everyone who has converted. In addition, Catholic membership has declined by 400,000 since 2008 alone, and more than 1,000 parishes have closed since 1995. Furthermore, there are 9000 fewer priests, or 8.5% drop since the 1960s, and over 3,400 Catholic parishes in the U.S. now lack a resident priest. Church attendance by Catholics in other parts of the world has become as dismal, or even worse. Data gathered from a Gallup poll, showed Church attendance for Belgium, France, England, Estonia, Finland, Iceland, Lithuania, Norway, Denmark, Sweden, Slovenia, Latvia and Austria to be less than 15%. Church attendance for the countries of Italy, Portugal and Slovakia were at 33%; whereas, Spain and Greece were 22-25%. The only two European countries in which church attendance exceeded 50% were Ireland and Poland.

In Luke (18:8) there is a question regarding faith on Earth *"But, when the Son of Man comes, will he find faith on Earth?"* The author of John (5:24) wrote *"Truly, truly, I say to you, whoever hears my word and believes Him who sent me has eternal life. He does not come into judgment, but has passed from death to life."* The first of the scripture readings indicates that proceeding the Second Coming of Jesus there will be a great loss in faith and according to the statistics, this has become a reality. Worldwide, on the average, only 20-30% of all Catholics attend church regularly. The unfortunate aspect about people not attending church is that it may cost them their salvation. Without faith there is no hope for eternal salvation, which is exactly what Satan is cultivating in our minds. If one does not acknowledge God throughout their life, how can they expect to be acknowledged by God on their day of judgment? Basically, God will say, "who are you?" Faith is a gift from God, and if people do not want to spend time with Him, why would He give them a gift they can care less about?

Many people accept God's existence, but don't go to church. They have their excuses; I don't go because I had a hard week at work and I just want a day to sleep-in; other excuses are it interferes with my playing golf, tennis, soccer, watching my favorite TV program, or going fishing, hunting, boating, to a ball game, etc. They allow all of these activities to be first in their lives, before thinking of their loving Father in Heaven. These people are "a bunch of ingrates" who live off God's blessings, but don't even give Him thanks. Are they any different from Satan? Satan also acknowledges God's existence, but he shows no gratitude or gives reverence to the God who created him.

Because there has been a great loss in faith, God's Spirit appears to be no longer coming upon as many young men to become priest, thereby causing the shortage of priest we have in today's world. These holy men are meant to consecrate the host to become the body of Jesus, and when we eat this spiritual bread, we become the children of God. Without them to do this blessing, we are eating nothing more than a wafer. If we are not going to church, why would God waste his Spirit on us? It is like someone buying a lot of food for a party, but nobody shows up to eat it, and party after party this goes on. So why buy food and waste it on people with no gratitude?

Are these not the signs of the end times? By God not having men to become priest, in essence he may be saying, "I keep trying to guide you, but you refuse me, so go ahead and see what it is going to be like when you are on your own." By reducing His presence; by lessening the number of priests to consecrate the host, more people will be more susceptible to Satan's subjugation. Since the 1950s, Satan has managed to convince about two-thirds of the world not to worship God. Even those who attend church may still not be living according to the teachings of Jesus.

Another abomination is for lesbian and homosexual ministers to give mass or sermons. God destroyed Sodom and Gomorrah. If he thought those people were abominations then, what makes these individuals think God will find them acceptable now? God loves men and women, but he does not love our sinful choices. All because someone goes to church, does not mean their godly. How many men and women go to church and treat it as if it were a punch clock, "I put my hour in"? How many men and women who go to church break the laws of God by stealing, fornicating, lying, hurting people, etc. on a daily basis? How many men and women who go to church backstab and lie about their coworkers, neighbors, and friends?

He will pardon us our sins if we sincerely ask for forgiveness, but if we choose to remain in sin, there is no absolution no matter how nice we appear to be to everyone. God can see through our façade. God is pure and will not allow a soul filled with uncleanness to enter into His kingdom. To be purified we need to go back to church, have faith in God, ask reconciliation for our sins, and to receive the Holy Eucharist. We must change our ways before He sends this period of tribulation into our lives.

Families (social upheaval)

One of God's commandments is "thou shall honor thy mother and father". Basically, you should obey your parents and do as they tell you to do without mouthing off, swearing, or disobeying them. It used to be that children, for the most part obeyed their mother and father. They used to say "okay dad", or "okay mom". However, like a general looking for his enemies' weaknesses, Satan found that he could break up 'the revered family unit'. One of his methods to wreck family unity has been accomplished by just having children becoming unruly and disobedient.

How could he do this? He uses television programming to subvert children's interaction with their parents and simultaneously teach them his ways of evil. He likewise has those disobedient youth, who have aligned themselves with him, to belittle and degrade anyone good; some of them who do want to be considered out-cast, react by modifying their behavior thereby affiliating themselves with the rebellious ones. His other approach to splinter the family would be to have one parent raise the son(s)/daughter(s), or for parents to have opposing views on child rearing. In either case, the end result is that these children will manipulate their parents and get whatever they want. He has made giant strides laying waste to the average family. In the 1950s, 72% of all families consisted of a mother and father; which was considered to be typical; however, by the year 2011 only 35% of all families were considered mainstream. That is more than a 50% decrease in sixty years.

The role of the parents has always been to provide stability for their children and to encourage them to make a better life for themselves. Parents need to be models for their children; consisting of going to church and by showing them true love comes by means of sacrifice. This includes forgiving after a wrong has been done. They also need to prevent their offspring from making wrong choices, and if necessary, if the child gets out of line, the parents should discipline them. Unlike years past when parents and schools actually had corporal punishment, this is no longer the case. It is not uncommon for today's youth to call Child Protective Services on their parents because they were punished. Schools also fear being sued by lawyers for reprimanding children. The result has become parents have become fearful of chastising their own children, and the kids know it.

In some Scandinavian countries, a parent who even yells at their child can go to jail, and there are parts of the world where spanking is illegal. A juvenile who is not discipline will believe that they can get away with anything they want in life. This may lead them to do drugs, steal and even kill. They have reached a point of being uncontrollable, and it is not uncommon in our society that adolescents are killing adults and other children.

The number of murders committed by children (5-18) during the past decade has leaped from roughly 1,000 to nearly 4,000 per year. On June 10, 2011, in Kansas City, a 5-year-old girl killed her baby brother for crying too much, and on November 8, 2008, it was reported that an 8-year-old killed his father with a gun. In the New York region of Queens, a 7-year-old was charged with killing a 2-year-old boy by throwing him off the roof. In Nassau County, New York, an emotionless 13-year-old admitted that he shot his mother dead. Moreover, in New York, a 15-year-old Bronx girl was indicted for murdering an infant, in a fire she set to her parents' house. In 1998, an 8-year-old girl was killed by a 14-year-old boy. In Texas, a teenage couple, who were formerly students at U.S. military academies, went to trial for their carefully plotted murder of a young girl, who had interrupted their love affair. In New Jersey, an 18-year-old high school senior delivered a baby while attending her prom, left the infant in the trash and returned to the dance.

These are only a few examples of disregard for human life, which have been escalating daily, since the 1980s. Some individuals might say these killings are normal and have always existed; it's just that they weren't reported before. Wrong, this is Satan's handiwork, and he is creating a whole army of these disorderly youth, who lack self-control and have an indifference to life.

Families have lost control over their children over the past fifty years; mainly the result of governmental laws instituted by politicians. These laws were imparted in the intellects of politicians, by none other than Satan. Why would Satan care about young people? He doesn't, but he knows these uncontrolled prodigies will enable him to eventually bring about his reign. Satan utilizes every available resource to achieve his goal. He continues to press his ways in the minds of our government officials, the same way he did when he twisted the minds of the Supreme Court Justices, who legalized abortion and got rid school prayers.

Has society forgotten that God tested the Jews by having them walk in the desert without the security of a city or home? This came about after they complained about not having any food and told Moses that they prefer to be back in Egypt as slaves. God went out of his way freeing them, and all He heard was their complaints. Yes, God further punished those unappreciative Jews by means of serpent bites; in addition, these rebellious people were forced to wander in the desert for forty more years until none of them were left to see the 'promised land'. Why? Because they could not accept God's authority and they believed that being the "chosen people", He would never castigate them.

Yet, we have people on Earth, who obviously think they know more than God and do not believe in rebuking an unruly child. The laws that prevent parents from punishing their children have actually created a generation of young adults who are oblivious to God's path towards righteousness. This path requires each and every one of us on Earth to exert self-control in our personal lives, so that we can enter into Heaven. People without restraint, and there are many in todays' society, will be the ones left behind in the final days of Earth to suffer the worst of God's punishments at the time of the tribulation.

Jesus warned us that Satan may appear as an angel of light to deceive even the elect. Satan has convinced those individuals who instituted these laws, to believe that they were doing what was right, when in reality, it's just the opposite. These laws created a host of children following in Satan's footsteps.

Social chaos is the result of not obeying the Ten Commandments, which include; do not kill, do not bear false witness, do not commit adultery, do not steal, honor your father and mother, do not take God's name in vain, keep the Sabbath holy, do not make images of god, or worship them, you shall not covet that neighbors wife, property, etc. Each one of these commandments is no longer being kept sacred and they have been put aside by people.

Because many people do not believe in God, the commandment about not committing adultery is no longer honored. Instead, men and women go out at night to perform these acts of betrayal; come home and act as if they did nothing wrong. It is a win, win for Satan, not only does he break-up marriages and parenting responsibilities, but he is collecting the souls of those sinners, who are lusting from their hearts.

God has been sending all types of signs warning us of our poor conduct and what will happen to us if we do not change our way of life. Put it in another way, it is like a judge who may give a person a chance to alter their lifestyles, so he may pardon them of their crime and allow them another opportunity to straighten their life out. However, if that same person continues to commit crimes, the judge will see that the criminal has no remorse and therefore he has no other choice than to place them in prison. God has been forgiving us of our sins, but if we keep ignoring His warnings, He will not tolerate our disregard forever and we will be in His prison.

Divorce (abandonment of faith)

It is written in the New Testament that the Pharisees wanted to test Jesus about the concept of divorce, so Jesus asked them, *"What did Moses command you?"* They said, "Moses allowed a certificate of divorce to be written and to divorce her." But Jesus said, *"For your hardness of heart, he wrote you this commandment. But from the beginning of the creation, God made them male and female. For this cause a man will leave his father and mother, and will join to his wife, and the two will become one flesh, so that they are no longer two, but one flesh. What therefore God has joined together let no man separate."*

God had a reason for mothers and fathers to raise children. His reason was to instill parental supervision and teach their offspring respect for others, but without these teachings; these adolescents will become immoral and susceptible to demonic direction. As mentioned, these broods have become disobedient to their mother, father, or whoever is raising them. Satan's desire is to end the cohesiveness of families, which can be easily achieved by leaving only one parent to raise the child; thereby lessening the ability of a single parent to control these unruly brats. Uncontrolled youngsters will be more receptive to Satan's guidance, and therefore, it will be easier for him to claim their souls.

Around the year 1917, at the time when the Blessed Virgin Mary was seen at Fatima, the divorce rate in the United States was <5%, by the 1950s this number increased to 20%, it continued to rise in the 1980s to 40%, then escalated to 50% in the 1990s. By 2010, the estimated divorce rate in the United States has been approximated to be 60% percent. Divorce rates in European countries have also increased: Sweden (54%), Denmark (44%), United Kingdom (43%), France (43%), Finland (43%), Russia (43%), Czechoslovakia (43%), Norway (40%), Lithuania (39%), Germany (39%), Portugal (26%) and Spain (15%).

There appears to be a correlation between the number of divorces and the percentage drop in church attendance. Many people, who raised families in the 1950s attended church and adhered to the teaching told by Jesus of *"It is unlawful for a man to divorce his wife"*. The Catholic Church forbade granting divorces and since many people in the 1950s followed the church's instructions, there were fewer divorces. However to circumvent this, if one doesn't attend church, or believe in its teachings; as it is today, one doesn't have to follow the rules. It is not much different than a child sticking his/her finger in their ear and yelling nah, nah, nah, nah, in order to pretend they don't hear what they are being told. Those wanting divorce only do what is pleasing to them, and if something interferes with their beliefs, they just ignore it. In our society if one doesn't like their spouse anymore, perhaps because they had an argument or maybe they found somebody prettier, they'll get a divorce regardless if they have a family responsibility. What is this lack of marital commitment doing to our society, or on our children?

We live in a self-centered generation that doesn't want to endure hardships, so their philosophy is "I'll just pick up my bags and leave; I don't want to deal with it." God wants us to be tested, and to show fidelity to our spouse in the tough times as well as the good. If we follow this commandment, we prove ourselves to be loyal to God as well. Satan proved to be unfaithful and was cast out of Heaven, so God is allowing us to prove our ability to be faithful on Earth first, and if we do, we will inherent Heaven as our eternal home.

Abortion (massacre of the innocents)

It is a blessing from God for a woman to have a baby. God has placed women very high in His eyes for their role of bringing life into the world. After all, Mary gave birth to His Son. Imagine, only God and women can bring life into the world. What an honor it is for women to be part of this miraculous event. However, the erosion of women's morals had become so great (relative to the year 1917), that many women from the years 1973-2011 look upon child rearing as a burden to their life styles, so they elect to have an abortion. In 1973, in the case of Roe vs. Wade, an evil process of murdering unborn children was legalized with a 7-2 majority decision by confounded United States Supreme Court justices. Now with this new freedom of choice women could focus on their careers, partying, and non-commitment lifestyles. Their thought would be, just get it out of the womb and let my life be free "I don't want this burden of a baby suffocating me". Prior to the year 1973 there were no abortion clinics, currently there are 682 clinics in America.

The National Right to Life reported that more than *fifty million babies* have been aborted in the United States since the 1973 Roe vs. Wade case. The vast majority of women having abortions have been mostly unmarried. Unmarried women accounted for 72.6% of the abortions in 1973 and 82.8% in 2004.

Those seven Supreme Court justices who voted for legalizing abortions have been responsible for more deaths than Adolph

Hitler's extermination of the Jews, communist and gypsies combined together during WWII. The number of abortions worldwide, since 1973, has been approximated to be *over one billion babies*. The world population at the time of Jesus Christ has been estimated to be fifty million people. Since 1973, there has been twenty times that number of babies murdered through abortion, as there were human beings at the time of Christ. In fact, it wasn't until the 1800s that the Earths' population even reached one billion people.

The act of murdering the innocent unborn child through abortion is an abomination in the making; it's a satanic ritual of sacrificing life to honor Satan. In a country such as China, where the government only allows a couple to have one child, the parents will determine through ultrasound whether it is a boy or girl. If it is a girl, many will elect to have an abortion, and hope the next pregnancy will bring them a boy. Similarly, in India many couples do not want a girl because they will have to pay a dowry upon her marriage, so they too determine by ultrasound, if they have a boy or girl in the womb, and have an induced miscarriage if it is a girl.

Each country has its own laws governing the number of weeks a fetus can live before being aborted. In general, many countries allow abortions' up to the first trimester, while it is not unheard of for a woman to have an abortion as late as the twenty-third week of pregnancy. Whether it is in the first few weeks, or first trimester of the pregnancy, the baby has formed and in 1974, a young doctor, who used to perform abortions said, "While doing a suction abortion, I found that the suction curette was obstructed by a torn-off fetal leg. So I changed techniques and dismembered the child with ring forceps and as I brought out the rib cage, I looked and saw a tiny, beating heart. And when I found the head of the baby, I looked squarely in the face of the human being that I'd just killed."

In a different clinic an ex-worker stated, "Sometimes *we lied*, a girl might ask what her baby was like at a certain point in the pregnancy. Was it a baby yet? Even as early as 12 weeks a baby is totally formed, it has fingerprints, turns his head, fans his toes, feels pain. But we would say "It's not a baby yet. It's just tissue, like a clot."

Another ex-abortion clinic worker described that during one process of an abortion, the doctor was trying to get the fetus out with forceps and as she watch the monitor; she saw the fetus try in vain to escape the forceps. These are actual terrifying images given by those who worked in clinics and saw the atrocities that were being committed.

If God thought the world needed to be punished in the early 1900s, how much greater His fury must be with the world we live in today, just with the issue of abortions alone. Satan has clouded the minds and hearts of these women, who don't want to be bothered with raising a child. He makes them believe that they are not taking a life; but in reality, the fetus in her womb has a head, torso, hands, legs, fingers, toes, and requires food to live. How can one say that this is not life? The Blessed Virgin Mary said, *"Many of these unborn children were supposed to save the world from what is about to happen"*.

Unwed mothers (misguided children)

The Bible condemns sex before marriage and can be found in the following: Corinthians 1 (5:1–4, 6:12–18), Corinthians 2 (12:21), Galatians (5:19), Ephesians (5:3), Colossians (3:5), Thessalonians 1 (4:3), Jude (7), and Hebrews (13:4). However, Satan has begun to seduce girls and boys of all ages leading them to a path of destruction. This trend of so many children having sex is not normal. We have strayed significantly away from the truth, and many babies born from these teenage children are often neglected, abused, given away, and raised by strangers. In some cases, these babies are murdered by their own mother. The problem becomes generation after generations of children are not being taught in the ways of the Lord, and the result is that their souls could tragically fall into the abyss. God sent us these commandments for us to follow, but without someone teaching them, we are lost.

Satan is going after and seducing younger and younger victims by placing lust into their minds and hearts. There is a sexual revolution taking place in the world, and although there was always a degree of sex outside of marriage, abstinence was more of the standard in the 1950s than it is today. It is not uncommon that young girls at the age of 12+ are having babies. Many years ago when life was difficult and many children were required to run a farm, it was common for girls to begin child bearing at a young age. However at that time, there were a large number of infant deaths during the birthing process, and many babies died due to the lack of proper medical attention.

According to the National Center of Health Statistics for Teenagers (data for 1950s-2000s), there were a high number of teenage girls giving births (9.5% of all births) in the 1950s, but most of these young women were married (~90%). However many teenage girls today giving birth are not married (80%), but represent ~33% of all births. Although this number of births appears down from the 1970s high of 44%, there was a reason for such a larger number of births to unwed mothers in the 1970s, compared to lower number of births to unwed mothers in the 1990s. As discussed, abortions are no longer illegal in the United States, so a greater number of pregnant teenage girls today elect to have an abortion; whereas, it was not possible to have one in the early 1970s.

Many teenage girls are getting pregnant due to peer pressure and seduction by evil. They want to be included with the popular girls, and one way is to be promiscuous; be like the girls in Hollywood movies depicting all the beautiful girls having the cutest boyfriends; attract boys by wearing super short skirts and at the same time wear thong underwear, thereby revealing all of their fleshy buttocks to arouse guys; be like the women who do pornography videos and make a lot of money by laying on their back engaged in sex; there have been reports of girls forming pregnancy packs where multiple teenage girls will get pregnant at the same time; some may even have an ultra-feministic attitude that says, "I can do anything I want to do and if you don't like it then go *@#k yourself". These may be a only a few of the reasons why young teenage girls are having sex, but no matter the reason they all are being manipulated by Satan.

Along with the daily inputs from the social environment, many young girls may come from divorced families, where there is no guidance at home. Even if there is guidance by parents, they may be very open-minded ones who don't care if their daughter has sexual intercourse "just make sure you have preventative sex dear..." It is not unheard of for girls to engage in oral sex on guys in the hallways at school. There are many examples of underage children having sex. However, the openness of sex has gone to the extreme when a 12-year-old girl and an 11-year-old boy began performing sexual intercourse in front of the class after the teacher had been called out of the classroom.

In the study by Christine Markham, Ph.D., assistant professor of behavioral science at the UT School of Public Health; Markham and colleagues defined sexual intercourse as vaginal, oral or anal sex. According to their research, by age twelve, 13% of students had already engaged in vaginal sex, 7.9% in oral sex, 6.5% in anal sex, and 4% in all three types of intercourse. The researchers said, "These findings are alarming because youth who start having sex before the age of fourteen, are much more likely to have multiple lifetime sexual partners, use alcohol, or drugs before sex, and have unprotected sex; all of which puts them at greater risk for getting a sexually transmitted disease (STD), or becoming pregnant."

The attitudes of boys and girls have changed over the past sixty years, and sex has become extremely opened for both sexes at tender ages. No wonder why there are fewer marriages, "why buy it, if you can get it for free" and the results are more and more babies are being born out of wedlock. It is bad enough for these babies to be raised by children, or a single parent, it is even more of revulsion when lesbian women have babies though sperm donation, or for married homosexual men to have babies by means of a surrogate mother. How fair is it to a child to be brought up in an atmosphere where both parents are the same sex? How can they make a choice? What an embarrassment they would have to endure at school and to be picked upon by the bullies. These innocent ones would suffer greatly due to the pervertedness of their parents. Is God not offended with all this licentiousness, sexual immorality and how we look upon our bodies as something to be plastered in a pornography movie or magazine?

Some may say God has sent a minor chastisement upon those who are sexually active and not married. The numbers of cases of Sexually Transmitted Diseases (STD) in the United States, developed since the sexual revolution, have been reported to be in the millions. Two-thirds of the STD's have been reported by young men and women between the ages of 15-24. The main types of STD's are HIV, chlamydia, syphilis gonorrhea, Trichomoniasis and Human Papillomavirus (HPV). There are currently sixty-six million cases of STD's, and it does not include homosexual men, or bisexual men with the Acquired Immune Disease (AIDS).

An article written by Dr. Darvin Smith stated that "AIDS, the dreaded sexually transmitted disease introduced during the late 80s, is receiving more attention than cancer. Since AIDS was first recognized in 1981, it has led to the deaths of more than twenty-five million people worldwide, making it one of the most destructive diseases in recorded history. It is a major threat to society and one of the most serious health problems the world has had to face. There are fifty-six million people worldwide affected with the human immunodeficiency virus (HIV). AIDS is primarily spread by homosexual practices, and it has become the major fear of the homosexual. AIDS is the now the leading cause of death in young men in USA."

During the times of Sodom and Gomorrah, homosexuality ran rampant and the people were wicked, however Abraham asked God not to destroy the cities if he could find at least "ten" good men. God agreed to Abraham's request, but there were not ten good men to be found; so both cities were destroyed by fire from the sky. Although they had fewer sins than we have in our society today, can we expect any different treatment by God? How much longer will He wait before he incinerates us with fire too?

Drugs/Alcohol (Satan's poison)

In Jesus's Parable of the Ten Talents, Matthew (25:14), he describes a master of a house going on a journey and before leaving; he gave three of his servants' ten talents each. After being gone for a while, he returned home and asked each one, what they did with the talents he had given them. Two of them made a profit while the third did nothing with the talents. The master scolded the one who did nothing with the talents, called him wicked and had him thrown out into the darkness. Satan knows that God has given us the ability to glorify Him through our works on Earth, but Satan wants us to waste our gifts. In doing so, we too will be judged as the wicked servant and our souls will be lost to damnation. What better way is there to waste a life than to have someone so focused on being 'high', that nothing else matters in their life?

The later part of twentieth century has been inundated with illegal drugs. Those who take them may, or may not become addicted to them, but if they become abusers, they may be following their path to destruction. Many believe that drug abuse and alcoholism are physiological addictions, but are they really? Perhaps these dependences can be attributed to demonic influences. Drug abuser personalities often changed during the course of being 'high' and coming off it; they become moody, depressed, angry, abusive, and irrational. They may batter their family (wife and children), or desert them to get their 'high' and they don't care if they live in the streets. The drugs mean more to them than family. They may become so far gone, their life appears irrelevant and they become suicidal.

    Throughout the years, the numbers of illegal drugs available have increased, and there are many types of drugs; some being natural while others being synthesized. Cocaine, heroin, methamphetamine, MDMA (also known on the street as 'ecstasy'), LSD, marijuana, PCP (Phencyclidine), Flunitrazepam (a.k.a. Mexican Valium or roofies) are a few of the drugs available to people. The drug problem in America began prior to 1900s, but it wasn't until after World War II when many soldiers found themselves addicted to morphine and other pain killers. It was if Pandora's Box of evil had been opened to the world, and many people began to descend into the abyss of drug addiction.

    According to the '2010' U.S. Department of Justice "National Drug Assessment", the United States alone has about 22.5 million users taking illegal drugs and another 15 million people suffering from alcohol abuse. According to the annual report of the UN International Narcotics Control Board (INCB), the estimated number of drug abusers worldwide in 2009 was between 172 million and 200 million people, and they spent 320 billion U.S. dollars annually to buy drugs.

    There are a number of crimes associated with drug addicts: homicide, robbery, abuse, prostitution, etc. The percentage of felonious crime caused by drug addicts can be very high; for instance, a 1981 New York study concluded that 40% of all homicides were drug related. In addition, the U.S. Department of Justice 'Drugs and Crime Data' reported in 2009 that 17-20% of all jailed inmates committed a crime to buy drugs, and this percentage has remained roughly consistent since 1991. The offences they committed were robbery, burglary, arson, larceny/theft and assault.

There are many unanticipated cost associated with drug addiction; such as, babies born addicted to substances and the neurological affects upon the fetus during gestation. These neurological affects may cause a lifetime of problems as the baby becomes an adult. Another unforeseen cost is when the addict comes off their 'high', they may become so depressed they will beat their spouse, parents, grandparents, children, and even commit murder. Even babies have been beaten, neglected and murdered by drug addicts during this period. In some cases, the abuser will often harm themselves. Some additional consequences of drug addiction are child abandonment, or having under-age children leaving home to avoid abuse. Those who leave home often start a life of crime, get involved with gangs, or in many females' cases, begin a life of prostitution.

Since there are drug addicts, there are individuals who sell these illegal drugs, and they have made it a lucrative business. They make so much money selling illegal drugs; they will often kill rival gang members, or anyone associated with these rival gangs to protect what they considered is their territory. In Mexico, there have been tens of thousands of people murdered, as result of drug violence, and the worldwide numbers may be in the hundreds of thousands. Illegal drugs are eroding society, just as Satan had calculated.

Those who take drugs are not only responsible for the crime they are committing, but also for the 'domino effect'; that is; they are indirectly responsible for all the crimes (i.e. murders) associated due to their drug addiction. Drugs steal the souls of human beings, many of whom may be giving up their eternal life just for a momentary thrill. What price is a soul worth, a gram of cocaine, a dime bag of marijuana, a pill or snoot full of vapors? Many souls have been sold for those bargain prices.

Drugs are not the only path that may lead a soul to hell, alcohol can also do it. The World Health Organization (WHO) estimates worldwide there are 140 million people addicted to alcohol. Alcoholics have many of the same problems as drug addicts. The negative aspects of alcoholism are 7.3% of divorces were caused by alcohol abuse, and 38% of all traffic fatalities. The leading cause of accidental death, are alcohol-related (National Highway Traffic Safety Administration, 5/27/99 press release). Alcoholics are nearly five times more likely than others to die in motor vehicle crashes.

Among sexually active teens; those who average five or more drinks daily were nearly three times less likely to use condoms, thus placing them at greater risk for HIV infection (American Journal of Public Health, 3/90). Almost half of college students, who were victims of campus crimes, said they were drinking or using other drugs when they were victimized. (C.R. Bausell, et al, "The Links among Drugs, Alcohol and Campus Crime").

There have been many reports stating that 73% of the felonies are alcohol-related, and researchers estimate that alcohol use is implicated in one-third to two-thirds of sexual assault acquaintance or 'date rape' cases among teens and college students (OIG, HHS, "Youth and Alcohol: Dangerous and Deadly Consequences," Washington, DC, 4/92). Alcohol related homicide and suicide accounted for 11% and 8%, respectively of these deaths. There are unfortunately innocent victims of pregnant female alcoholics' whose fetus can develop Fetal Alcohol Syndrome (FAS). FAS is a pattern of mental and physical defects develop in a fetus, and is in association with high levels of alcohol consumption during pregnancy; perhaps after birth, the baby will have a difficult adult life due to the alcohol as a fetus.

Alcoholics are also victims of Satan, who is trying to claim their souls through their immoral behavior while under an intoxicated state of mind. Satan is actively trying to destroy families either through drugs, or alcohol. It is not unusual for an alcoholic to spend their entire paycheck on drinks, and end-up not being able to pay the household bills; consequently causing marital problems. Many of these families get divorced, and the children suffer the most consequences by not having the stability of both mother and father to help raise them.

The question of whether alcoholism, and drug abuse are physiological, or demonic caused may be answered by an organization called alcoholics anonymous (AA). This organization recognizes that for an alcoholic to overcome their addiction, each abuser must pray and place their faith in God. Only God can defeat Satan and demonic forces; perhaps this is why this organization realizes that drug, and alcohol dependency may not be physiological addictions, but rather demonically driven.

Homicides (a path of disobedience))

A few of the Old Testament Commandments are thou shalt not kill, steal, or lie. Have we forgotten what these commandments are? Satan's approach to seal humanities doomed fate is step by step, and he wants to be gruesome about it. Humanity has always regarded murder as being the highest offences against God because it takes away a human life; something that can never be replaced due to each individual being unique. There have always been murders; the first recorded one was when Cain killed his brother Able, due to jealousy. After a long period of violence in our world, humanity was slowly becoming more civilized and manslaughter had become less acceptable. However, as we had passed through the twentieth century, the world has become filled with more violence. It is not unheard of in the twentieth or early twenty-first century of adult men, or women not only committing carnage on each other, but also on children.

We live in a world filled with killing: fanatical religious killers, serial killers, contract killers, cult killers, crime killers and mass killings. According to the twentieth Century Atlas-Worldwide Statistics of Casualties, Massacres, and Disasters; there have been 8.5 million homicides in the world, from the years of 1900-1999 alone, not including another 227,000 murders in the United States since 1999. Drug cartels are massacring hundreds of people each day in Mexico, and South America; so that they can maintain their control of the drug trade. The trend of murdering in today's society has gone well beyond what one would call typical behavior.

The number of worldwide mass murderers has skyrocketed in the twentieth century. Between the years of 1900-1950, there were 24 mass murderers, and from the years1950 to 2011, there have been 125 mass murderers, with the majority of them being committed since 1980. The number of mass murderers is beyond what mathematicians would consider a statistical average, even after adjusting for the world population growth. Demons can direct both our behavior and thoughts. They can even cause individuals to perform mass slayings not only for pleasure, but in a sadistic fashion. One of these sadistic murderers was gay and would entice other gay men to his apartment; at which point, he would kill those who had been lured, dismember them, and eat their hearts. Many victims of mass murderers have been female; this includes not only elderly women, but young girls too. Many of them had been raped first, and then murdered by these possessed individuals. A former decorated sergeant killed 14 family members, including young children and three toddlers. Another grizzly murderer even raped a 5-year-old girl before killing her. Other inhuman murderers would decapitate their victims and put their body parts in a refrigerator. Another sadistic killer wanted to start a race riot in the United States, and to instill fear in the public, he would have the words "Helter Skelter" written on the victims' walls from the blood pouring out from their stab wounds. Those who encountered this man said that when one would look into his eyes, it appeared that he was actually possessed by a demonic being.

Adults are not the only ones committing mass murderers; young adults have also committed these atrocities. In 1999, two Columbine High School students embarked on a massacre shooting twelve students and one teacher. They also injured twenty-one other students directly, and three people were injured while attempting to escape. After their slaughter, they committed suicide.

Other disturbing trends of murder, which are frequent in today's society, are infantile deaths. Between the years 1970 and 1990, the official infant homicide rate rose dramatically from 4.3 to 8.4 infant deaths per 100,000 residents. This rate continued to increase during the 1990s and by the 2000s the infant homicide rate was 9.1. Almost one infant homicide per day was reported in the year 2000, with a total of 349 deaths. Many cases involve parents shaking their child to death, while other murders are more hideous. Most of them are parents killing their children. In 2011, a 29-year-old mother from California cooked her 6-week-old daughter to death in a microwave. In a parallel case that took place in 2005, a 26-year-old Ohio mother, in a drunken state, intentionally placed her newborn baby in a microwave oven and cooked her to death. There have been two more similar reports, one in Texas and one in Virginia, where young mothers have done the same thing. Are these acts not demonic?

Child killings are taking place at unprecedented rates. According to an article written by Charles Montaldo, in the Crime/Punishment Guide; he stated, "The American Anthropological Association had reported that more than 200 women kill their children in the United States each year." Three to five children a day are killed by their parents. Homicide is one of the leading causes of death of children under age four. A few examples of child killings include a 29-year-old Alabama woman who killed her 2-year-old adopted daughter in 1999; a 20-year-old woman covered her 4-day-old son with duct tape resulting in his death; a 25-year-old Arizona woman killed her 4-year-old son in 1989; a 34-year-old California woman killed her two daughters, age 4 and 9 and her son, age 8 in 1994; a 42-year- old California woman killed her three sons, ages 5, 8 and 11 in 1999; a 33-year-old California woman murdered her four sons, ages 4, 6, 7 and 14 in 1996; a 49-year-old California woman killed her grandchildren, ages 4 and 6; and a 29 year-old Pennsylvania woman killed her 7-year-old daughter. And the list goes on and on. Is this normal for these women to commit these ghastly murders? Recall that it was earlier written that Satan will continually use an evil tactic on everyone. This is proof of it.

Can you see him? All of these depraved and 'possessed' individuals committing these ungodly acts are being driven by Satan. Can you see now Satan's footsteps in our society? The number of other murders in the twentieth, and early twenty-first centuries committed by the hands of individuals have been so great, it would difficult to document them all. These murders are being committed not only because of the age old reasons of greed, theft, jealousy and insanity, but they are also for sheer pleasure. It is truly a time in history where Satan has managed to control the thoughts and actions of many, many people, and the only way to prevent from becoming one of his possessed victims, is to pray.

Why does Satan have so much power over us today? Maybe we have left ourselves opened to Satan's suggestions because we have rejected God's protection. If we don't worship God, we are telling Him that we can live life on our own without his input. As the Virgin Mother had told the visionaries "pray, pray, pray". It is no wonder why she has been saying this, just look at the downfall of humanity.

Suicide (surrendering all hope)

Only God has the right to take a life, and we are told to endure our crosses until the end. Many people have found it difficult to carry their crosses in life, and they get so depressed, that suicide seems their only option to circumvent additional misery. Worldwide suicide rates have increased 60% in the past sixty years; regardless of the world population growth. It has increased from 10 suicides per 100,000 people to 16 suicides per 100,000 people. There currently are ~1.2 million worldwide suicides per year, as compared to the 1950s when world suicide number were less than 260,000.

There are many forms of suicides: pact-suicide, murder-suicide, mass-suicide, euthanasia and self-harm suicide with many others reasons for suicide. On April 15, 2009, fifteen hundred debtor Indian state farmers committed mass-suicide after their crop failure. Newspaper headlines in 1978 showed at Jonestown, Guyana the bodies of nine hundred members of the Peoples Temple, which was founded by a cult leader. It was a murder-suicide where woman and children were killed by drinking Kool Aid laced with cyanide. In another incident of mass suicide, the leader of "Heaven's Gate" convinced thirty-nine of his followers to commit a pact-suicide because he believed a spaceship, following the Hale-Bopp Comet, would take them to their "new world destination".

Throughout the Middle East on almost a daily basis, there are suicide bombers that kill themselves along with as many people as possible. They are told of receiving a great reward for doing this, and they would be in Heaven with Allah. There are many, many murder-suicides where an individual will take other persons lives and then commit suicide.

The pressure of the world is getting to many people, who are unable to cope with life. They have become prime targets for demonic forces that tell them; there is no hope to continue on with your suffering; end your life and you will be in paradise today. However, we are told in the bible "to endure to the end", and yet many people believe suicide is the answer to their problems, when in truth it is only the beginning of them.

Satan wants to prevent any glory going to God, and many people do not understand we glorify God by enduring the hardships of life. Jesus carried his cross, both figuratively and literally throughout his life until he was crucified. God expects us to be like Jesus, to carry our crosses loaded with difficulties until the bitter end. By committing suicide, we have committed murder on ourselves, and since the dead can no longer ask God forgiveness, these souls may have lost their eternal reward.

As can been seen from what has been written, there has been a great deal of social decay in our society over the past one-hundred years; all of which is demonically architected to capture our souls. Souls are falling into Hell like the rain falls from the skies and it has become a deluge. How much longer will God wait until he destroys the planet and the source of our sins?

Chapter 6

A World Fallen Into Moral Decay

Stealing (A path leading to destruction)

One of God's commandments is "thou shall not steal"; however the amount of stealing throughout the world has increased faster than United States budget deficit in the past ten years. Where have integrity, honesty and trust gone in our world? It is no longer just stealing from banks or other people; stealing has progressed in many ways. There is identity theft where individuals open up credit card accounts with somebody else's identity. Afterwards, they purchase as much as possible before the creditors close down the account. The poor victim has to deal with the creditors to clear up their credit rating. There is white-collar theft done by investment managers. Some of them have bilked millions or even billions of dollars from their investors. One investment broker had a Ponzi scheme that managed to defraud fifty billion dollars from his investors.

White-collar crime is not solely committed by investment managers, but also by doctors, CEOs, corporations, and even trusted members of the community. There are doctors, who fraudulently bill Medicaid hundreds of millions of dollars for services never performed on patients. There are corporations stealing billions of dollars from the U.S. government, as they unjustifiably overcharge for products, or in some cases never deliver the products to the government. As reported by the Los Angeles Times (November 4th 2003), criminologist Jeffrey Reiman, a professor at American University, estimated that the total cost of white-collar crime in

1997 was $338 billion and that was using conservative numbers, and he believed that the cost were most likely much larger.

In comparison, the FBI estimated in 2002, typical crime committed by individuals; such as, robbery, burglary, larceny-theft, motor vehicle theft and arson came to only $18 billion. This is less than one-third of the estimated $60 billion The Enron Corporation cost its investors, pensioners and employees through their dishonest financial disclosures in 2001. The Enron Corporation is an example of a dishonest corporate leader having employees falsifying earning statements, to make a favorable depiction of the company's performance to the Wall Street analyst. These falsified statements enabled the stock price to go up; resulting in the top executives receiving $1.4 billion from salaries, bonuses, and stock options. However, a year later, the stock tumbled from $83 to $1 per share, with the investors losing their savings, once the fraud was realized.

Another example of trusted CEO's doing white-collar crime was the head of WorldCom, who became very wealthy from the rising price of his holdings in WorldCom common stock. However, when the corporate financial earnings began to look poor, he reportedly had the books falsified to make the company look profitable, thereby he would benefit from his stock holdings. In spite of this, after an internal auditor began asking questions about WorldCom's questionable bookkeeping practices, it was discovered that any apparent gains obtained from their improper accounting, were actually an $11 billion loss. WorldCom went bankrupt, investors lost their money, and all the employees lost their jobs and pensions.

The cost of white-collar corporate crime reached far beyond the investors and employees of the company. For example, scandals during the period of 2001-2003 resulted in a significant drop in some corporate stock prices affecting not only the investors, but also cost the New York State's economy about $2.9 billion. In addition, they caused the state tax revenues to be cut by $1 billion, and decreased the New York State pension fund value by $9 billion.

It has been estimated that since the year 2000, American corporate scandals have added up to losses of more than 200 billion dollars. Sin cascades like an avalanche and eventually everyone gets hurt. The overall result from these scandals causes not only revenue income to be diminished for investors, but reduces pension portfolios, detracts from employment, and shrinks tax revenue. It is estimated that more than a million workers lost their jobs through these scandals. Some families broke up, and their children suffered with little to eat or no clothing to wear. White-collar crime goes well beyond theft of money; the most detrimental part of this type of crime is how it had affected the livelihoods of millions of people.

It was not long ago when people would admire the accomplishments of individuals such as CEO's or presidents of companies. These men would be examples that mothers and father would say to their children, "You too can make it to the top by working hard". Now many people look at these men as heartless and selfish individuals who have sold out their souls to the devil for money, and this is exactly what they are doing. They downsize their company and get rid of high paying jobs or reduce the workforce, so that they can keep the financial earnings looking good for the analyst. In return they get their big bonuses for keeping the stock price up, but at what expense?

How many families have had to suffer from their greed? In Matthew (6:19) Jesus said, *"Do not store up for yourselves treasures on Earth, where moth and rust destroy, and where thieves break in and steal, but store up your treasure in Heaven."* Similarly, in Matthew (16:26) Jesus said, *"What good will it be for a man if he gains the whole world, yet forfeits his soul?"* When Judas turned Jesus over to the Pharisee's, they gave him thirty pieces of silver, but that money cost him his soul.

In another parable regarding wealth (Luke 16: 19–31), *a rich man lived a luxurious life, well fed, wearing fine linens; while a poor man named Lazarus lived in rags, was covered with sores, and ate the scraps that fell from the rich man's table. When they both died, Lazarus went to Heaven and enjoyed his inheritance; the rich man on the other hand, went to Hell. When he saw Lazarus in Heaven, he requested Abraham to send Lazarus to him with quenching water. Abraham answered it was impossible and furthermore he told the rich man, he had enjoyed life on Earth, whereas Lazarus suffered, and now both have received their just eternal rewards.* Can these corrupt corporate CEOs, who have negatively affected millions of people lives, expect a fate different than Judas or the rich man?

Cyber-criminals (ghostly thieves)

Cyber-criminals are like thieves in the night, they come into peoples' homes and when everyone is a sleep, steal their possessions. After all, credit card theft it's not really real a crime, is it? Criminals no longer have to steal using guns, now with current electronic devices; cyber-criminals can steal from people, businesses, banks, and governments throughout the world, in the comfort of their own homes using computers. Prior to the 1990s and before the Internet was invented, criminals would have to personally approach their victim (whether it be a person, a home, a bank, an armored car or a train) using a weapon to steal from them. With the onset of the Internet and other inventions, thieves can now steal without their victims' knowledge.

Credit card theft is one such crime, and is the fastest growing type of fraud in the United States. In 2008, about 9.9 million Americans were reportedly victims of credit card/identity theft, an increase of 22% from the number of cases in 2007. In addition, the Federal Trade Commission (FTC) estimates credit card theft costs consumers about fifty billion dollars annually. With today's technology, a thief can walk past someone holding a radio-frequency-identification- device (RFID) and scan credit card numbers in a wallet or purse. These individuals, who steal this information, do not feel any remorse about purchasing items with these stolen credit card numbers. For these thieves, this is free and easy money; their consciences do not bother them, for this type of crime hidden from the eyes of the law. There is so little honesty left in the world that individuals are afraid to turn their back on anyone, in the fear that their identity will be stolen.

According to the Internet Crime Complaint Center (IC3), they have logged its two-millionth consumer complaint alleging online criminal activity in November, 2010. IC3 is in a partnership between the FBI and the National White Collar Crime Center and went operational in May of 2000. It took seven years before IC3 received its one-millionth complaint in June of 2007, but half the amount of time to receive its two-millionth complaint. This indicates that that cyber-crime is rapidly on the increase, and no one is safe.

Cyber-crime is not only an America problem; there are cases of cyber-theft throughout the world, in Russia, China, India, and Europe. Cyber-crime is now costing the UK $43.5 billion and the world about $1 trillion. A web security company, Trend Micro, believes that during the first half of 2010, Europe had surpassed both Asia and the Americas as the top region for producing Internet-based threats. In India, cyber-crimes have been increasing by a whopping rate of 100% each year; causing people to lose confidence in online shopping. The top countries in the world that have the greatest number of cyber-crime victims are China and India, which stand in the first and second positions.

Cyber-criminals can even get into military data bases of governments, where they can steal secrets, and potentially cause a war. In Canada, there was an unprecedented cyber-attack on the Canadian government's Defense Research and Development, making it the third key department compromised by a hacker. The attack, apparently from China, gave foreign hackers access to highly classified federal information, and forced the Finance Department and Treasury Board to get off the Internet.

We are being tested each day by Satan. He wants us to yield to him by any means; whether it is by stealing, lying cheating, killing, etc. Many are falling into his snares and it can be seen that our world is filled with lawlessness. The numbers of crimes committed show that Satan is winning, but it also means that for those who have not succumb to him, they should prepare for the Lord's Day. Those individuals who commit cyber-crime have forgotten God's commandment of "thou shall not steal". Satan on the other hand has convinced them that cyber-crime is not stealing, when in reality it is one of the worst forms of theft. Cyber-crime can be likened to demons; we can't detect their presence, only see the results of their actions and that many people get hurt due to them.

Sex crimes (seduction by Satan)

Sex has always brought out the worst in a human being's behavior, and it is probably the best weapon that Satan uses to destroy humanities' relationship with God. Sex was meant for procreation of our species, but it is now being over-used as a pleasure avenue by the masses. People have become consumed with indulgences of the flesh. It has not only generated a multi-billion dollar per year industry, but has caused a huge increase in the numbers of sex crimes. Much of this lewd behavior may be largely attributed to the amount of pornography available; such as, the publications of Playboy, Hustler or Penthouse magazines.

The invention of VHS and DVD players also enable an individual to play pornographic movies at home. If one doesn't own either of these two pieces of electronic inventions for watching pornography; they can always go into the local XXX-rated movie theater to watch sexual intercourse, or even go to a club where women perform sexual acts on stage. The types of perverted sex that can be seen on a DVD player or an adult channel can be acts of lesbianism, multiple partner sex, bestiality, sex with children, etc.

The numbers of women, who permit themselves partaking in sex videos or to be photographed nude and/or engaged in acts of genital penetration, are increasing each year. Men, who constantly watch pornography, believe all women are nymphomaniacs. The logic of these men becomes "if they what to get it on, hey, I'll just have to oblige them", so they go out seeking to satisfy their lust at any cost. Some men may find themselves so desirous with the intimate partaking of female flesh, they will rape, kidnap women to become sex slaves, spend hours on company time scouring Internet pornography, seek out prostitutes, and even engage in pedophilic activities with under-aged girls. They have become the pawns of Satan, and they will do anything to satisfy their desire for sex.

The numbers of sex crimes have increased throughout the world, and the exact numbers cannot be fully accounted for because many are never reported to the authorities. For example, in Europe, a new form of lucrative sex industry is termed white slavery. Young white women are kidnapped, and forced into prostitution. In Hamburg; Russian prostitutes have been smuggled in by criminals who desire to increase the profitability of their business. Police have found Russian women are kept as slaves by criminals, who want a greater share of the sex market. Sex slavery is not only found in Russia, but also in, Germany Czechoslovakia,

France, Poland, and most other European countries. Many women are forced into slavery as a means to make money for the criminal elements.

Although slavery ended in the United States during the 1860s; women forced to engage in unwanted sex for cash has become an ungodly act to make money. The U.S. "Trafficking in Persons Report" stated that from 2010-11, these sinful acts are in 184 countries with estimates up to 27 million people laboring in sex-bondage around the world, and even children are forced into prostitution. Here in the United States, the State Department estimated that between 45,000 to 50,000 people were annually trafficked to the U.S. for 'sexual exploitation', between the years 1997-2010. Within that short period of time, over 650 thousand women and children have had a man forcibly perform an erotic act on them without their consent.

Men, who partake in indecent exposure in front of a woman, or touch the personal parts of a woman's body without her permission and are caught, become listed as sex offenders. According to the annual report on Multi-agency Public Protection Arrangements (MAPPA), involving Whales and England, the proportion of registered sex offenders per 100,000 of population rose from 40 individuals in 2003, to 46 by 2004. This represents a 15% change in the number of offenders within a year. The British Home Office Statistics showed similar results, in which there were 24,572 offenders in England and Wales on the register at the end of March 2009 compared with 21,413 in 2008. This represents a steady 15% increase in the number of registered sex offenders each year. The numbers of lustful flesh crimes are showing a consistent upward trend.

The numbers of these crimes reported in Sweden during the year 2009 were 15,700 sexual offenses, which was an 8% increase over the year 2008, and of those offences 5,940 were rape. It was also reported in April 2009, that crimes of the unsolicited seduction in this country had risen by 58% since 1999. A '2009 European Union study' concluded that indeed Sweden has one of the highest occurrences of reported rape in Europe.

Other indications that sexual crime is increasing throughout the world can be found in a new study conducted by the Medical Research Council (MRC). They determined that 500,000 rapes are committed annually in South Africa. A '2010 South African government study' reported that more than 37% of men have said they had raped a woman. Also, nearly 7% of the 487 men surveyed said they had participated in 'gang rape'.

Unwelcomed sexual acts are also prevalent in America. The FBI's "Index of Crime in the United States" (ICUSA) cited that forcible penetration increased 418% from 1960-1999. The U.S. National Crime Victimization Survey (Bureau of Justice Statistics, U.S. Department of Justice, 1996) reported that a woman in America is raped every two minutes. In 1995 there were 354,670 women who became victims of unsolicited sex and/or sexual assault. In 2009, a major television news network report that nearly 90,000 women reported cases of uninvited sex in the United States during 2008, and it's estimated that another 75,000 cases of forcible sex went unreported.

Adults are not the only ones who are being accused of violent sexual acts in the United States. On June 9, 2007, MSNBC reported that the number of children under 18 accused of rape, and nonviolent sex offenses rose from 24,100 in 1985 to 33,800 by 2004. That corresponds to a 40% increase in sex crimes by juveniles over a period of nineteen years. Meanwhile according to the American Humane Association (AHA), the total number of overall child sex abuse cases rose steadily from 2,032 incidents in 1976 to 22,918 in 1982, and reached 323,400 incidents by 1999, all of which represents a 1590% increase during that time-frame.

Inappropriate behavior offenses are likewise being committed by educators. Both men and women have been convicted of having sex with their under-aged students. In a five year study by the Associated Press from 2001 through 2005, an average of five hundred educators faced disciplinary or criminal action following allegations of sexual relations with students. Typically, men are associated as being the ones engaging in sex with students. Uncharacteristically, more than ten percent of these sexual encounters with under-aged students were committed by female teachers.

In other parts of the world including Africa, the Middle East and Asian countries have also reported a significant rise in sexual crimes; most in particular rape, in which the victims include girls, as young as, 10-years-old. It was reported that in 1996, there were 1,071 reported sex abuse cases in Malaysia; predominately a Muslim nation, and is evidence that it too is not immune to Satan's seductions of the flesh. Reported cases of rape in Malaysia grew to 1,323 by 1997, a 23% increase from the previous year, and the upward trend looks to be continuing. It was also reported, by the local media, that during a four month period, there is at least one sexual assault a day. Similar data is also reported in India, a country filled with people of Hindu and Buddhist faiths. Satan clearly has no bounds or respect for any faith.

All of this data reflects that throughout the world, crimes of the flesh have been escalating since 1960. Regardless of one's religious belief, Satan is collecting the souls of individuals committing sex sins, and he is leading them into his kingdom of Hell. He is including the souls of not only men and young boys who seek sex by committing rape, but also those men who feel that they can make money by kidnapping and subjugating women in to a life of fornication. Only God knows the number souls that have been and will be lost by those seditious acts of the flesh.

Pedophiles (fallen men)

No one is immune to Satan' temptations and the pious are the most likely candidates to be under a constant barrage of attacks. Some of the most disturbing sex crimes are by Catholic priest, who have molested children. Bishopaccountability.org acknowledges that thousands of Catholic clergy and religious personnel have raped and sodomized tens of thousands of children—perhaps more than 100,000 children since 1950. The real tragedy is that most of these victims could have been saved by the bishops, if they had addressed the actions of suspecting clergymen. Since the 1990s, there have been nearly 15,000 survivors who have spoken out, and through their accounting the church has been able to recreate an in-depth picture of these improper incidences by the clergy.

Many sexual encounters by priest may never be known to the public. According to the U.S. Bishops Council, there have been 5,948 priests accused of sexual child abuse between the years 1950-2010. This number represents 5.4 % of the 109,694 priest who had served since the 1950s. Half of the number of these priests accused of molesting a child were only one-time offenders;

however there were 149 priests who committed ten or more offences. Of the victims, approximately 81% were male, of which 51% of them were between the ages of 11 and 14. In 2005, it was reported at the U.S. Conference of Catholic Bishops, "The crisis is not yet over because thousands of cases are still being reported." Most of the alleged incidents were between 1965 and 1974."

When Satan seduced these holy men of God, it was if he had stolen the Crown Jewels of England. These were good men of God, trusted by their parishioners, and for these priest to be under Satan's power became too much for many Catholics, so they left the church. This was Satan's intentions from the beginning, not only did he test the clergy, but he also tested the faithfulness of the parishioners.

In Matthew (13:3–8), Jesus gave a parable about the sower, *"The farmer went out to sow his seed. As he sowed, some fell along the road and it was trampled underfoot and the birds of the sky devoured it, other seed fell on the rock and as soon as it grew it withered away because it had no moisture, other fell amid the thorns, and the thorns grew with it and choked it."* The people who left the church are like the seed that fell on the rock and withered away, they accepted the word of the church and God, but withered away when there was hardship within the church. Satan clearly understood this would be the reaction of people, and they would leave the church in droves and lose their faith in God. It was said by Sr. Lucia that the third Fatima message would be best understood if it was opened in the 1960s, which has turned out to be the beginning time for the persecution in the church.

Gangs (a path to hell)

Gangs come from every race, nationality, creed and color. A list a few gangs in the United States include: White, Russian, Hispanic, Black, Irish, Native American, biker, Middle Eastern and many other diverse gangs. In 2006, there were approximately 785,000 active street gang members in the United States; between 25,000 to 50,000 gang members (Zetas) in El Salvador and Mexican drug cartels may have as many as 100,000 foot soldiers. More than 1,000 gangs were known to be operating within the UK in 2009.

The FBI estimates the size of the four Italian organized crime groups to be approximately 25,000 members in the U.S., with as many as 250,000 affiliates worldwide. The Russian, Chechen, Ukrainian, Georgian, Armenian, and other former Soviet organized crime groups or "Bratvas" have many members and associates affiliated with their various sorts of organized crime, but a rough number has not been estimated. The Yakuza are among one of the largest crime organizations in the world; in Japan, as of 2005, there are some 102,400 known members and Hong Kong's Triads include up to 160,000 members in 2001. It was estimated that in the 1950s, there were 300,000 Triad members in Hong Kong. Gang members have become the pawns of Satan.

According to the FBI, some 20,000 violent street gangs, motorcycle gangs, and prison gangs with nearly one million members are criminally active in the U.S. today. Many are sophisticated, well organized; all use violence to control neighborhoods and boost their illegal money-making activities, which include robbery, drug and gun trafficking, fraud, extortion, and prostitution rings.

The Gainesville, Florida police department wrote, "Gangs are neither just a big city nor inner city problem, nor are they a problem of a particular race or culture. Gangs cross all ethnic, racial, socioeconomic, gender and geographic boundaries. They bring fear and violence to neighborhoods, traffic in drugs, destroy property, involve youth in crimes and drive out businesses. Gangs pull teens away from school and home into a life of violence. One of the scariest aspects of gang violence is its often indiscriminate and unpredictable behavior. Gang members have been known to kick, punch, hit, and sometimes kill their victims. People who are simply in the wrong place at the wrong place often get hurt. If gangs or gang members are in your school or neighborhood, you know it".

Some of the statistics about gangs are as of 1995 gang problems had been reported for all 50 States; including the District of Columbia, for about 700 counties and 1,500 cities and towns. The number of municipalities reporting gang problems rose from 201 cities in the 1970s to 1,487 cities by the mid-1990s, an increase of 640%. Some may argue that this growth reflects population increases for the cities. However, the population of these 'gang-problem' cities rose from 36.5 million in the 1970s to 131.5 million in 1995, an increase of 260%; whereas, gangs are growing more than twice the rate of population growth.

This expansion in gangs may be attributed to the fact that many of the members often come from broken homes, where males are reared in fatherless households. Without a father, who can act as a role model, these youths go out and seek those males who can, and gang membership played a vital role in learning and practicing the characteristics and attitudes of male adulthood. Gangs are not the answer for our youth; instead they're one of the problems.

These last two chapters on social and moral decay are evidence that humanities' rate of degeneration is nonlinear. Satan has extended his influence far into our daily lives and we are being gobbled-up like a busted bag of seed being eaten by birds. It's a feast day for them, as for Satan too, and to believe that this world is not being consumed by demonic forces is incomprehensible. The world is crumbling faster each and every day. There is more and more violence, more and more greed, everything is moving towards greater extremes of evil.

Honesty, benevolence, integrity, and trust have been thrown out the window in our society, and we have replaced these good ethical qualities with lying, killing, greed, lust, divorce, violence, disobedience, licentiousness, selfishness, etc. All of these makings were prophesized by Paul in his Second Letter to Timothy. We are in his prophesized times now; it is no longer a future event, and it can all be attributed into a world falling away from God.

The results from all of this decay will not stop with just social deterioration. They are other signs for the end of times as well. There have been and will be an enormous upsurge in the amount of evil leaders who will follow Satan's path of killing; all paramount for the end times to begin. Eventually nature will have her turn and make life on Earth unbearable; for there will be hunger, plagues, misery, and death for all of humanity. This will only be scratching of God's fury upon the planet. When His wrath really begins to unfold, nature will alter the face of the Earth.

Before all of this devastation unfolds, we will have been given preliminary signs. It will be like the time when God made a covenant Abraham; the word of God was quiet and sounded like the whisper of the wind. Likewise evil has been quiet, barely heard, as it slowly slipped into our world, but soon it will soon become loud and boisterous and when it does, nature which had been silent will awaken and begin to rebuke mankind.

The initial minor weather aberrations will become greater and greater and the sound of a constant loud clap of thunder will be God's mighty fist coming upon the world. Nature will be tenacious in punishing us unceasingly until we reach the very last days. She will take away our ability to eat and drink as part of our punishment. Then in those days, the worst will take place with multitudes of wars, floods, fires, droughts and a barrage of unpredicted astronomical anomalies will strike the surface of the Earth. Be prepared, these things are coming very soon!

Chapter 7

A World in Chaos

Economy (a day's wage for a loaf of bread)

The bible clearly specifies that in the end times, there will be unprecedented economic distress throughout the world. In Matthew (24:7), Jesus said, "*Nation will rise against nation and kingdom against kingdom and there will be **famines**...*" In the book of Revelation (6:5–6), "*I heard what seemed to be a voice in the midst of the four living creatures. It said **a ration of wheat costs a day's pay**, but do not damage the olive oil and wine.*" These biblical prophecies indicate that the price of food will be so high that it will require one whole day of work just to feed the family, and many other people in the world will starve because they have no way of paying for food.

Desire for wealth has become rampant, so much more than ever, over the past thirty years. There have always been selfish people, but now it has spread like a fever contaminating whoever it touches. There are persons who have manipulated the stock market and received large amounts of money for doing so. CEO's had their human resources lay-off workers to improve the company's profits, so that they could get big bonuses. Banks and mortgage companies falsified personal income data for unqualified borrowers; in order to provide them mortgage loans, and hedge fund managers drove up the prices of commodities, etc. There are many reasons for the worldwide economic collapse that started in 2008, but materialism was the driving force behind it all.

The economic collapse has had an effect upon everyone in the world. People barely have enough money to buy the necessary staples in life. Charities are seeing a decrease in monetary contributions from those who used to give, and currently those contributors are struggling themselves. A great deal of their donations would have been used to provide relief for the hungry and now with fewer donations, the people hardest hit by high food prices come from nations already suffering famine.

An article written in the economiccollapse.blog stated, "Right now in 2011, countries such as; Somalia, Ethiopia and Kenya are experiencing the worst drought conditions that they have seen in sixty years. Tens of thousands of African families have abandoned their homes to desperately search for food and water. Hundreds of thousands of farm animals have died because of the drought... Every single day, thousands of African families head to Dadaab, the biggest refugee camp in the world, which was designed to hold 90,000 people, but now has over 360,000 people. At this moment there are over 30,000 hungry people, who are outside the fences hoping to be admitted and by the end of the year there may be more than a half million people living in Dadaab. Even worse the United Nations indicates that food shortages may affect ten million people in the region, and if the drought continues there could be mass starvation in Africa by 2012."

Furthermore, other organizations and news agencies have been written reports stating that more than three billion people live on less than two dollars a day and over the past year, the global price of food has risen by 37%, and since 2004, food prices have gone up by 240%. According to the '2011' UN Food and Agriculture Organization report, approximately one billion people throughout the world go to bed hungry every single night, and every 3.6 seconds someone starves to death with three-quarters of them being children under the age of five.

According to the World Food Bank, forty-four million people around the globe have been pushed into extreme poverty since June, 2010 due to rising food prices. They blame the current global food crisis to have been brought on by the greed of the wealthy. In the land of plenty (America), according to data from the U.S. Department of Agriculture, there are 42,389,619 Americans who received food stamps, as of August 2010, a 17% rise from the previous year. Food stamp recipients have increased 58.5% since August 2007, before the recession began.

Another source indicating of forthcoming food shortages comes out of the U.S. Department of Agriculture, which said that corn reserves will drop to a 15-year low by the end of 2011. The United Nations reported global food prices hit another new all-time high in the month of January 2011. They are projecting global food prices will increase by another 30% before the end of 2011. Much of these food prices have been exasperated by acquisitive commodity hedge fund managers, scorching heat, or unprecedented flooding that devastated the 2010 winter wheat crop in Australia.

The Northern Hemisphere has roughly six months for crop production, providing sufficient food for the world and the converse is true for the Southern Hemisphere. Disruption of food production in either hemisphere will affect the amount of food for the world; such as, the winter of 2011 in Brazil where food production has been substantially hampered because of flooding. Russia, one of the largest wheat producers on the entire globe, is still feeling the effects of the 2010 summer's scorching temperatures, and it is actually importing wheat this winter to sustain its cattle herds.

China is busy preparing for a severe long-lasting drought that is projected to have a huge impact on several provinces. The Chinese state media reported that the eastern province of Shandong is dealing with the worst drought it has seen in two hundred years. The negative impact resulting from this drought is that these provinces are no longer able to produce the approximately two-thirds of the wheat grown in China. The drought is causing the Chinese to import nine times more corn than the U.S. Department of Agriculture originally projected for them for the year 2011.

Another factor causing food shortages in the world is the amount of topsoil being lost at unprecedented rates. There was an article written that one-third of the world's cropland is losing topsoil faster than new soil is forming through natural processes.

Other reasons for these shortages can be attributed to U.S. ethanol subsidies, which utilizes almost one-third of all corn grown in the United States, for the use as a gasoline supplement. Because of subsidies from the government, farmers make more money selling corn for ethanol production than for food use, causing the price of corn to go up. Countries in the Middle East are finding themselves having to seek out the basic food staples from other nations. In order to save water, Saudi Arabia stipulated that all wheat will be imported by the year 2016.

Water tables all over the globe are being depleted at an alarming rate due to 'over pumping'. Data from the World Food Bank indicates there are 130 million people in China, and 175 million people in India being fed with grain grown with water that is being pumped out of aquifers faster than it can be replaced. Many nations that were previously huge food exporters are now importing a greater amount of their food. All of this is driving up the prices for staples such as wheat, corn and soybeans. The UN is projecting food prices will continue to rise rapidly throughout the year 2011. According to the UN's Food and Agricultural Organization, the global price of food hit a new record high in December. The previous record high for food prices was in June 2008.

A 2011 Forbes article reported that since June 2010, corn is up 94%, soybeans are up 51% and wheat is up 80%. Food requires fertilizer to make it grow and without it, the yields will become extremely unsupportive of being able to feed the world. The cost of fertilizers has almost tripled in the past ten years and at some point, the world could experience a very serious fertilizer shortage, thereby driving food prices up ever so much more. Compounding to this problem are the commodity speculators, who are also driving up food prices owing to the atypical worldwide weather patterns over the past several years. Both Northern and Southern Hemispheres have experienced traumatic weather; whether it is extreme heat, cold, rain or drought. Farmers are unable to get there crops planted, or in some cases the crops fail due to lack of water or too much water.

The price of oil may be the biggest factor for food price hikes. Food production and transportation to market is very heavily dependent on oil. Ravenous speculators have been driving up the price of oil, and subsequently our entire system of food production becomes much more expensive. If this trends continues and there some individuals who indicate that the price of oil will go up to $120 a barrel from the current $87 a barrel, then food prices and shortages will continue.

All of these food shortages and price hikes are causing unrest throughout the world. In April 2008, Egypt had riots due to the cost of wheat going up. There have been reports that violent economic riots are now being reported in Algeria, in Chile and in Mozambique. Food shortages and price increases are also causing political unrest in other nations such as India, Bangladesh and Indonesia.

It is evident that there are many reasons why there are food shortages, and that these shortages will become so staggering that only the rich will be able to eat; forcing people to riot, murder, and steal. As food becomes harder to come by, it may force countries to start wars with other countries to acquire what resources they can; potentially propagating wars that would involve the whole world. Much of these food shortage hardships could have been avoided, but greediness residing in the hearts of many has brought the world closer to the inevitable final conflict between good and evil.

It appears that rider of the black horse, from the Book of Revelation (6:5-6), has begun to make his ride throughout the world, bringing about starvation to many people, and those who may not be hungry today, may soon find that they will be envying the scraps thrown out to feed the pigs.

Chapter 8

A World Lead by Evil Men

Middle East (A place of concern)

The Middle East is essential in ascertaining that the end times are approaching. The bible states that Israel will be attacked by an army consisting of 200 million men. This part of the world at the turn of the twentieth century was a group of countries led by Shahs, Sheiks, tribal leaders, and in some cases puppet leaders, placed in those positions by outside interests. The majority of these desert nomad people proved not to be any threat to anyone at the time. They were poor and lacked any army that would pose a threat to Israel. However, after World War II and with the evolution of oil revenue, many Middle Eastern countries fell into the hands of oppressors, who used the oil proceeds not only to be living in luxury, but also for acquiring military equipment to maintain their control of power. They built up their armies with warplanes, tanks, missiles, and the latest hand held weapons (i.e. Russian AK-47 military assault rifles and rocket propelled grenades, known as RPGs).

These dictators suppressed their fellow countrymen so much that in the late twentieth and early twenty-first centuries many of these tyrants were being overthrown, by unsettled young people. One such country, Iran, fell into the hands of the Grand Ayatollah Sayyed Ruhollah Mostafavi Moosavi Khomeini, who was Iran's religious leader and politician. He led the 1979 Iranian Revolution, which saw the overthrow of the Shah of Iran, Mohammad Reza Pahlavi, by sacrificing 20,000 people lives, most of whom followed the Ayatollah.

In the wake of the revolution, and by means of a national referendum', Khomeini became the country's Supreme Leader. A number of years later, another hard line cleric named Ayatollah Seyed Ali Hoseyni Kahmene'i took over the country. He rules the country with an iron hand, and totally supports their current president Mahmoud Ahmadinejad, who has hawk-like sentiments towards Israel. A major danger regarding many of these clerics is they are caught-up with the ideology that any non-Muslim should either convert to Islam and every Jew should die.

The Middle East has been transformed throughout the twentieth and early twenty-first century, and it has become indeed a plaguing and unsettling place. There are individuals who want to create chaos in the region, and they would like to see Israel destroyed. These once desolate and arid Middle Eastern countries having little, if any, persuasion towards the overall direction of the world at the turn of the twentieth century, have become powerful players on the political stage. They can topple governments and destroy economies simply by manipulating the price of oil. They may even be capable of acquiring weapons of mass destruction.

The current Iranian President Mahmoud Ahmadinejad is totally anti-West and anti-Semitic. He has openly declared that all the Jews should die, and he has sponsored terrorist activities against Israel and western countries. He has provided the Palestinians, who oppose an Israeli State, with weapons and thereby has contributed to the multiple clashes between the Palestinians and Israeli's. President Mahmoud Ahmadinejad has been seeking, with the help of Russia, to isolate fusible nuclear fuel. Many speculate it will be used to build a nuclear bomb. Even countries like Pakistan, which have a nuclear arsenal, can be a threat to Israel provided they are overthrown by Muslim extremists who maintain President Mahmoud Ahmadinejad philosophical beliefs. These radicals may even provide him with the nuclear bomb, so it is important that Pakistan does not fall into their hands.

All eyes from the West are scrutinizing the nuclear program going on in Iran. Acquisition of such a device, through any means by Iran, would mean precarious and prophetic times for the people of Israel. It can be certain a man such as President Mahmoud Ahmadinejad would attempt to destroy the Jews with a nuclear weapon. If Iran does possess a nuclear weapon, Israel may perform a pre-emptive strike resulting in World War III.

If other revolutionaries continue to overthrow their governments and replace them with religious extremists, it could fulfill the time written in the Book of Revelation foretelling a time when Israel is surrounded by its enemies. As these extremist take control of their oppressor governments and fill themselves with hate, sponsored by Satan himself, evil will tempt them to declare war on Israel. However, when they set their eyes on destroying Israel, God will show his glory against those evil men with judgment and death following.

Evil dictators of the twentieth century (Satan's henchmen)

Jesus said, *"At the end of days, there will wars and rumors of wars."* Satan has limited time to enact his strategy against the church and all of humanity. He requires the use of those individuals accepting his beliefs to achieve his objective. He corrupts through power and throughout the twentieth century, the number of evil dictators have increased multi-fold. These sadistic men have been responsible for the murder of hundreds of millions of people. Vladimir Lenin, a communist, who engineered the Russian Civil War, became head of Russia and was responsible for the deaths of nine million Russians. After his death, Joseph Stalin took over Russia in1927, and is responsible for approximately twenty-five million Russian and Ukrainian deaths during a period of seven years (1932-1939).

Ismail Enver Pasha, an Ottoman Turk, was the perpetrator of the Armenian Genocide. He was Minister of War and was accountable for the deaths of 1,200,000 Armenians in 1915; 350,000 Greek Pontians plus 480,000 Anatolian Greeks from 1916 to 1922, and more than 500,000 Assyrians from 1915 to 1920.

Adolf Hitler was responsible for the deaths of over six million Jews that died in Nazi death camps, by either being worked to death, gassed, shot, or cremated in ovens. Overall, through his policies, Hitler is responsible for more than 66 million deaths during WWII (1939-1945). Benito Mussolini, Italy's Fascist dictator during the years 1924-43 had designs to establish a new Roman Empire.

He set out with desires to conquer parts of Northern Africa and during his campaign 300,000 Ethiopians and Libyans died.

Hideki Tojo was the Prime Minister of Japan from the years 1941-44. He was responsible for the attack on Pearl Harbor where over 2300 American soldiers and civilians died. He also is responsible for all the deaths of the American and Japanese soldiers, and also for more than five million civilians. Most of the civilians killed were Chinese and Filipinos being murdered by his soldiers; whereas, two hundred fifty thousand Japanese civilians died from the atomic bombs dropped by the Americans in a response of Hideki Tojo war policies.

Mao Ze-Dong, Chairman and leader of China from 1949-1976, is responsible for 48-79 million Chinese deaths, with most of them dying (38 million) from his "Great Leap Forward Program" during the years of 1958-61. Kim II Sung, communistic dictator of North Korea, is accountable for the deaths of more than 1.6 million North Koreans, who died in purges and concentration camps.

In the year 1971, Idi Amin became president of Uganda; backed by Libya's Muammar al-Gaddafi and the Soviet Union, he managed to exterminate 500,000 of his people. Another dictator named Pol Pot became leader of Cambodia in the mid-1970s. During his time in power, he forced urban dwellers to relocate to the countryside to work in collective farms and labor projects. The combined effects of forced labor, malnutrition, poor medical care and executions resulted in the deaths of approximately 21% of the Cambodian population. In all, an estimated 1,700,000–2,500,000 people died under his leadership.

Saddam Hussein, President of Iraq from the years 1979-2003, caused hundreds of thousands of his own countrymen to die through genocide extermination. Furthermore, hundreds of thousands of Iraqi soldiers died in wars with Iran and NATO. In all, he may be responsible for one million deaths.

Libya's Muammar al-Gaddafi has been in power since 1969 when he had overthrown King Idris in a bloodless coup; afterwards, he established the Libyan Arab Republic. During his time as head of Libya, and during the 1990s he masterminded and financed a brutal war that left 300,000 Liberians dead in West Africa's Sierra Leone. Another dictator, Slobodan Milosevic, President of Yugoslavia and Serbia (1992-99) was a longtime communist and through his genocidal policies during the Bosnia-Herzegovina War (1992-1995), 100,000 people died.

The list goes on and on with these murderous oppressors killing more than 100 million people throughout the twentieth century; in addition, they have initiated swarms of wars on every continent in the world and had extracted riches for themselves at the expense of their people. "Many of these dictators rose to power after World War II and were able to maintain their authority by the use of military weapons; obtained predominantly from communistic Russia, or China. As foretold, these countries are spreading their evil intentions throughout the world.

Extreme Religious Fanatics (followers of darkness)

Although the exact number of people killed throughout the twentieth century by religious fanatics is not known, the numbers are in the tens of thousands. It is a fundamentalist theological way of thinking surmounting to nothing more than chaos, Satan's best ally. There are two types of fundamentalist religious fanatics. One type believes they have properly interpreted the Koran and all other renditions of the Koran are wrong. Therefore, they believe that in order preserve their interpretation, it is permissible to kill anyone teaching the other interpretation. The other extremists believe all other religions should be prohibited and therefore these fanatics want to kill Christians, Buddhist, Jews, and all Westerners.

One of these extremists, named Osama Bin Laden, had the latter belief and he sponsored terror throughout the world. Neither he nor those who follow him can be called the children of God; instead, they are the children of Satan. They have carried out terror plots in Europe, the Middle East, Africa and the United States, killing innocent people.

Osama Bin Laden master-minded the blueprint for fellow terrorist to crash commercial jets into the buildings located in the predominately Christian West (The United States of America). On September 11, 2001, they had carried out their initiative to hijacked four jet airliners on the same day; whereby three jets crashed into buildings (one each into the Twin Towers in New York City, and one into the Pentagon in Washington, D.C.). The fourth aircraft crashed into a field in Pennsylvania, after the passengers had taken back the plane from these extremist. Everyone died on those airplanes and so did many people in the buildings; including many firefighters and policemen, who were attempting to rescue those stuck in the building as they collapsed. These terrorist caused the deaths of more than 3000 innocent people.

The people in the Middle East cheered on the streets to see all of this horror on TV committed by fellow Muslims. How ironic that these same Muslin terrorists, who come from a religion that supposedly promotes peace and proclaims self-control over the flesh, went out the night before to party and drink at strip joints. How were these men able to pay for the training lessons required to fly these large jets? Who paid for all carousing they did? Was it sponsored by an extremist Middle East government? Iran?

In actuality, Osama Bin Laden caused more than 40,000 deaths. Those killed in the airplanes and Twin Towers and those who died as a result of the NATO led Afghanistan War; as a result of the Taliban's refusal to turn Osama Bin Laden over to the Americans.

The religion of Islam is taught by clerics, who are supposed to lead and teach Muslim people how to live a holy life, but some of these clerics had become extremists and have declared a jihad 'holy war' on all people who are not Islamic. Since when does God; maker of Heaven, Earth, and all that is seen and unseen, need anyone's help to kill in His name?

These fanatical zealots have plotted in Europe to either plant bombs, or use suicide bombers on subway trains to kill as many people as possible. They have strapped suicide vests on men, women, and children. They tell them to blow themselves up along with as many other individuals as they can. These suicide bombers are under the belief they will go directly to Heaven "a lie", but to those who plot and commit these acts will not be forgiven by God. The trend of using suicide bombers and terrorist to make attacks on western cultures continues and many Muslims, whom have adopted this concept, embrace it as their jihad. They don't realize that this jihad is being directed by non-other than Satan himself, who delights in promoting murder, and more murder. For those murders who do his bidding, they will become his in Hell.

Overall, turmoil continued throughout the twentieth century and these sinful men slew many good men and women in our world. Eventually there will be a time when wickedness has become so widespread; it will be dangerous to even go outside your house. The twentieth century has been filled with every form of iniquity, and each day we will hear of more murders, disasters, wars, acts of greed, terrorist attacks, political upheavals, socio-economic distress, etc. It is impossible to list the number and amount of atrocities conspiring in this world on a daily basis. Evil has touched the heart of every man, woman and child and has distracted us from the truth. There remains only a remnant of true believers, who accept the word of God and live by his laws of love. It is hard to comprehend, not only the amount of evilness in our century, but how accepted it has become.

We live in an age where one man can kill hundreds, or thousands of people using relatively simple modern day weapons of war. Sinful men will continue to acquire these weapons and misuse them for personal gain. The Holy Bible clearly stipulates, through messages by the prophets that our current society is living in the last days, and we should be vigilantly looking for the coming of Jesus.

Some signs shall be seen in the state of the world's condition; such as the numbers of these evil leaders; other signs will be of nature, and finally there will be signs are from Heaven. Some of the signs from Heaven have/and will arise through prophets, and yet still other signs will be super natural. The super natural signs will be observed by a few privileged chosen ones, who will bear the burden of trying to convince the masses that God, or His Son, as well as the Virgin Mary has spoken to them. These chosen ones will come under much scrutiny, ridicule, and will carry the heaven cross of remaining faithful with the daunting task of convincing people to convert before it is too late.

Chapter 9

Signs upon the Earth

As the world gets closer and closer to the end of times, the world will not only be filled with chaos from moral and social deprivation, but devastation through the elements. Everything is linked and it will all come together at the final end. The Earth will begin to revolt against mankind's wonton disregard for the planet, causing widespread annihilation. It will be as if the Earth wants to eradicate the disease, called mankind, and year after year there will be greater numbers of floods, earthquakes, hurricanes, tornadoes, etc. The world will be so torn-up that it will be hard for farmers to plant their crops, and even if they did, the crops may suffer from drought, flooding, frost and pestilence.

Those countries exporting foods may no longer be able to do so in the future, because they would lack sufficient resources to feed their own people. This will cause other countries that import food to no longer be able to feed their people. There will be widespread famine with riots ensuing and perhaps collapses of governments. This could further escalate into wars with neighboring countries, and before long it could erupt into World War III. It may not happen all at once, but as each year passes these incidences will grow and grow, like a cancer, until no country on Earth will be able to handle all the disasters. They will have become financially bankrupt attempting to save their countries means of life.

Are we getting closer to the end? Jesus said there will be signs in the skies and this includes changes in weather, brought upon the Earth either by mankind, or by God. When the storm of the century, hurricane of the century, or earthquake of the century develops every year, or every other year, it will be the sign that we are approaching the tribulation.

Earthquakes

It has been written, that at the end of time the world will go through convulsions like a woman in labor; one of the convulsions will be in the form of earthquakes. The United States Geological Service (USGS) measures the size and number of worldwide earthquakes and records them in a data base. In the past twelve years, there has been an average of sixty earthquakes per day in the world.

A study by Marilia Tavares and Anibal Azevedo on seismic activity concluded that the numbers of earthquakes have been increasing since the 1950s. They found that solar maxima, coronal mass ejection, coronal holes and Earth's magneto-sphere all alter seismic activity. The numbers of earthquakes are not only rising, but the data from USGS show they are growing in magnitude. The average number of earthquakes with magnitudes greater than 5.0 throughout the 1970s were 1534/yr., however in the early 2000s this number jumped to 1933/yr. This represents at least a 26% increase in the number of earthquakes during that time period. As of mid-August 2011, there have been 1805 earthquakes with magnitudes greater than 5.0. This would extrapolate to over 2900 earthquakes by the end of 2011, a whopping 50% increase over the number of 5.0 magnitude earthquakes experienced in the 1970s. Jesus warned us (Matthew 24:8), as we approach the end of time, there will be great earthquakes throughout the world. It is as if God has begun to shake the foundations of the world as a warning to humanity, and there will be a lot more shaking yet to come, if we don't revert back to our beliefs in Him.

Volcanoes

In Matthew (24:29–30) Jesus said, *"After the tribulation of those days the sun will be darkened and the moon will not give its light and the stars will fall from the sky and the powers of the heavens will be shaken. And then the sign of the Son of man will appear in Heaven… and they will see the Son of man coming upon the clouds…"* It is also written in the Book of Revelation (Chapter 8:5), *"Then the angel took the censor, filled it with coals from the alter and hurled it down to the Earth. There were peals of thunder, rumblings, flashes of lightening and an earthquake."*

What Jesus depicted and that which was written in the Book of Revelation describes the effects of volcanic explosions. Volcanoes have caused devastation upon the Earth on a numerous occasions; they have the power to change our climate in an instant by spewing out enough ashes to block the sun's light from entering the Earth. When a volcano erupts, the Earth rumbles, there are flashes of lightening, and there is thunder. There have been well known eruptions throughout our history; one famous volcano was Mount Vesuvius located in Pompeii, Italy. Pompeii was a decadent city filled with rich Romans, who practiced many forms of sexual sins. Mount Vesuvius erupted in 79A.D. killing all of the inhabitants. It was as if God had become fed up with their immoral behavior and wiped them out with fire and ashes.

In 1816, a weird combination of solar activity, and the eruption of Mount Tambora resulted in a year throughout the world with no summer. It snowed in the months of June, August, and September killing off the meager crops that managed to grow, in the less than hospitable climate. The best known volcanic eruption in the modern era was Krakatoa. It was among the most violent volcanic event that culminated in a series of massive explosions during August 26–27 in1883. The sound from the eruption traveled 3000 miles, and over 120,000 people died either from the explosion, or the following tsunamis. The average global temperatures fell by as much as 1.2°C (2.5°F) the following year. Weather patterns continued to be chaotic for years, and temperatures did not return to normal until 1888. More recently in the United States, Mount St Helen blew up in 1980, and devastated 230 square miles of land. In 2010, Iceland's Kalta volcano blew enough ashes into the upper atmosphere to force 100,000 flights to be cancelled.

These volcanoes are powerful and can cut out light, destroy hundreds of square miles of land, stop travel, and reduce food production by causing the summers to cool so much that crops will barely grow. Although these volcanoes are powerful, none of them have the capability to cause total catastrophic destruction upon the Earth with the exception of super volcanoes. They have a force of destruction that is thousands of times more powerful than normal volcanoes.

Super volcanoes are constructed differently than normal volcanoes in that they contain a chamber of molten magna lying just below the Earth's surface and these chambers are hundreds of square miles in size. If they erupted millions of people would be killed; enough ashes would cover the circumference of the globe, block sunlight and prevent the crops from growing. The gases bellowing from these volcanoes could generate acid rain capable of burning human flesh. Afterwards, the temperatures would drop so much that snow would fall in the summer months. An unexpected event could be potentially happen if several super volcanoes erupted simultaneously; this being, they could potentially knock the Earth off its precessional axis.

At this moment there are super volcanoes located in the United States' Yellowstone National Park; Lake Toba in Sumatra, Indonesia; Pacana Caldera in northern Chile; Cerro Galan, in Catamarca Province Argentina; Kikaki Caldera - Osumai Islands off Japan and Campi Flegrei in Naples, Italy. There are also sisters to super volcanoes; such as the ones at Laacher See Lake, located in Koblenz, Germany and Russia's Kamchatka super volcano; both of which haven't erupted in millions of years. They are all showing signs of activity and have been coded orange, one step away from the next level at which time they will erupt. Yellowstone National Park, home to a massive super volcano, has been monitored by the United States Geological Service. They have reported that the surface of the caldron has risen 170 feet during the past fifty years indicating that it too may become active. Across the remainder of the planet, these giant dormant volcanoes are slowly but surely awakening from their long period of dormancy.

A catastrophic event that could precipitate several simultaneously eruptions of these super giant volcanoes, would be if the Earth experienced a massive strike by an astrological body such as a comet or asteroid. Recently a midsized meteor about the size of an aircraft carrier barely missed hitting the Earth, by about 23,000 miles. Had this meteor had hit the planet; the force of the impact could have been enough to arouse any of these super volcanoes. Scientists say it is not a matter whether a meteor is going to hit the Earth, but rather when. Has God designated one of these meteors to hit our planet and fulfill that which has been written in Revelation? Only God knows.

Solar flares

The sun provides essential life to the planet, and may play a special role in the future of mankind. At Fatima, witnesses' said that the sun appeared to be falling to the planet, and when everyone cried out; it receded back to its place in the heavens. Was this a preface of what will happen to Earth in the near future? Our Lady of Fatima told Lucia, *"when you see a night illumined by an unknown light, know that this is the great sign given to you by God that He is about to punish the world for its crimes, by means of war..."* On January 25, 1938 a remarkable aurora borealis display was visible across Europe. That illumination was the result of massive solar flares; it signaled the onset of WWII, which actually began in March 1938 after Germany annexed Austria.

If the sun was a sign precipitating a world war, could it also signal another catastrophic event? If so, the sun may currently be motioning other calamitous times may soon arrive upon the planet. On June 8, 2011, the New York IB Times reported "the biggest solar flare in four years observed by NASA was unusual, and further spectacular activity of the sun will likely create a display of northern lights called aurora borealis." The scientific world has agreed that the sun will exhibit a high amount of solar activity from the years 2012 through 2013, but what type of activity? Could the sun shoot out massive flares and disrupt the electrical grid, transportation and communication? Could the sun throw out some form of mass, and hurl it towards the Earth?

In Revelation (8: 7), "When the first angel blew his trumpet, there came hail and fire mixed with blood, which was hurled down to the Earth. A third of the land was burned up, along with a third of the trees and all the green grass. This scripture passage specifies "fire was hurled down" to the Earth, causing one-third of the Earth to be burnt. One possible way to create so much fire would be for the sun to unexpectedly eject a large amount of solar plasma. Should this mass hit the Earth, it would cause widespread fires throughout the world, in fulfillment of the scriptures.

Climate Change

Not all of the end times signs upon the Earth are contributed solely to catastrophic earthquakes and volcanic activity, but some of them could be precipitated by mankind itself. Global warming in the past sixty years has reached epidemic levels, due to mankind's' callous disregard for nature. Scientists are pointing at the industrialization of the world for generating carbon dioxide gases at a rate faster than the planet can consume them. This gas comes from many sources; such as, the emission of gasoline powered vehicles, burning coal, emissions from trucks, and any vehicle that uses hydrocarbon fuels. As the population of the world increases and people travel more, the pollution will become suffocating.

Another contributor to global warming is the rain forests are being disseminated at an unprecedented rate. Human beings are destroying them, as they encroach farther into the rain forests for farming and living. The trees are essential to absorbing carbon dioxide, and converting it into oxygen. Without trees, there is no way to prevent the atmosphere from filling up with greenhouse gases (CO_2). Greenhouse gases retain the heat in the atmosphere, and act just like a lid on a pot of warming water. By preventing heat from escaping, both the pot of water and planet heat up faster.

Researchers are predicting as the planet gets warmer; the polar ice will melt, causing the ocean levels to rise. The combination of higher water levels and more warmth will result in more hurricanes in the Category 5 range having sustained winds in excess of 156mph and waves greater than 18ft. There will also be an increase in the EF5 category tornadoes with wind speeds between 261-318 mph, and damage paths as wide as 3300ft. The oceans will rise to unprecedented levels causing many major cities to be under water. Weather patterns could change so much that cities adjacent to rivers would be flooded; affecting the farmlands throughout the world. In addition, the jet stream may permanently shift, and cause fertile land to dry up through extended droughts.

Hurricanes

Woe to mankind! Human beings have carelessly ignored the planet and believe they can do whatever they want to it without penalty. They have discarded the Earth's warnings; the world temperature has warmed, resulting in more and stronger hurricanes. It will be as if the four angels in the Book of Revelation, who normally would hold back the winds, will instead release them in the form of hurricanes and tornadoes. Hurricanes are an awesome display of power and can be extremely destructive by generating winds in excess of 150mph for sustained periods of time and can move huge amounts of water on to the land.

According to a '2010' article written in the USA today weather, "The number of hurricanes that develop each year has more than doubled over the past century, an increase associated to global warming." A researcher, at the National Center for Atmospheric Research in Colorado, conducted a study, and reported there have been substantial increases in hurricanes over the last century. These increases are closely related to higher sea-surface temperatures found in the tropical Atlantic Ocean. The researcher found the average number of hurricanes jumped sharply, from 3.5 per year for the first 30 years of the twentieth century, to 8.4 per year since the beginning of the 21st century. Over that time, the Atlantic Ocean surface temperature has increased by 0.65 degrees.

Researchers at the Georgia Institute of Technology and the National Center for Atmospheric Research (NCAR) reported that the number of Category 4 and 5 hurricanes worldwide has nearly doubled over the past 35 years. The increased strengths of the hurricanes are being attributed to an increase in global sea surface temperatures. Professor Peter Webster and three students from Georgia Tech's School of Earth and Atmospheric Sciences studied the number, duration, and intensity of hurricanes and typhoons (hurricanes in the Pacific Ocean) between the years 1970 to 2004. They found that during the 1970s, there was an average of ten Category 4 and 5 global hurricanes per year. However from 1990, the average number of global Category 4 and 5 hurricanes almost doubled to eighteen per year.

Tornados

Woe! Woe to mankind! The powers of the winds are growing more abundantly each decade. Many countries in the world get tornadoes: Europe, Russia, Africa, South America, Australia, Japan, India and New Zealand, but it is America that gets 75% of all them in the world with Canada coming in second at 5%. Unlike hurricanes that attack from the oceans, tornadoes are unpredictable; they travel on the land and can destroy cities in a few minutes. They generate violent rotating winds with speeds ranging from 100-300mph. The diameter of a tornado can vary between a few feet up to a mile, and its track can extend from less than a mile to several hundred miles.

According to data from TornadoHistoryProject.com, the average number of tornadoes per year for each decade in the United States has been: 1950 (201), 1960 (616), 1970 (653), 1980 (866), 1990 (1133), 2000 (1075), 2010 (1282). As of May 24, 2011 they have recorded 1243 tornadoes, representing a 600% increase over the average number of yearly tornadoes occurring in the 1950s. The average number of April tornadoes has steadily increased from 74 per year in the 1950s, to 163 per year in the 2000s. The number of confirmed EF0 tornadoes (65-85 mph wind speeds) has steadily increased to more than 800 a year from less than 100 per year. The spring tornadoes of 2011, hit hard in the southern and midsections of the United States, and destroyed whole cities with many lives being lost. There were 875 confirmed tornadoes in April 2011, triple the previous April high of 267 in 1974. The average number of tornadoes in May during this past decade has been 298, with the record number of tornadoes for May being 542 in 2003.

The highest recorded number of tornadoes in a single year was 1,819 in 2003, which is a 900% increase over the average number of yearly tornadoes from the 1950s. The numbers of tornadoes are steadily increasing each decade, and they are becoming fiercer and deadlier. The financial economic cost of tornadoes is in the tens of billions of dollars, and each year that number grows, putting more stress on the fragile economy.

Flooding

From the Book of Revelation (8:13), *"...I looked and heard an eagle flying high overhead and cry out in a loud voice, "Woe! Woe! Woe to the inhabitants of the earth, because of the trumpet blasts about to be sounded by the other three angels."* It is bad enough that the Earth is experiencing more hurricanes, more tornadoes and more earthquakes now the number of floods are increasing each year. The numbers of catastrophic floods per decade over the past sixty years have been: 1950s (6), 1960s (4), 1970s (3), 1980s (4), 1990s (12), 2000s (21). So far, since 2010 there have been nine floods, which would extrapolate out to a staggering sixty devastating floods by the end of the decade. In the United States, an extremely snowy 2010-11 winter and an abnormally wet spring flooded most of the lands adjacent to the Mississippi River.

These lands are crucial to food production in the United States, and many farmers were unable to plant their crops this year, costing the country billions of dollars. Similarly, the spring of 2011 in China, resulted in a series floods for their central and southern parts of the country. The floods were caused by heavy rain that inundated portions of twelve provinces while leaving other provinces still suffering a prolonged drought. A total of over 36 million people have been affected with direct economic losses of nearly $6.5 billion dollars.

In 2010-11, floodwaters washed through Australia's third-largest city, and submerged entire neighborhoods. The damage from the flooding has been likened to the aftermath of war. The flooding started in late November, and has covered the same amount of area as the countries of Germany and France combined. It was Brisbane's worst flood since 1893, and has shaped up to be Australia's costliest with damage estimates around $5 billion. Also, in 2011, Rio de Janeiro and other parts of Brazil were flooded by record amounts of rainfall; this has become the worst natural disaster in Brazil's history.

In 2010, Sri Lanka experienced one of its worst flooding in its history, cause by unceasing rains. Over one million people have been affected. There were also floods throughout Europe in 2010, with areas in both France and the United Kingdom being under water. Ireland and in the United Kingdom; especially in Cumbria County, had its share of floods in 2009, causing extensive damage. In 2008, India's Bihar region experienced one of the worst and disastrous flooding in its history. The Koshi River changed its course and devastated areas, which hadn't experienced floods in many decades. The flood affected over 2.3 million people in the northern part of Bihar. The Bihar region also flooded in 2007, and was described by the United Nations, as the worst flood in the living memory of Bihar. In 2006, there was relentless flooding in Bulgaria, Romania, Germany Serbia, Hungary, caused by record snowfalls and rainfall.

Just as the numbers of hurricanes, tornadoes, earthquakes and volcanic activity have become more active; each year catastrophic floods are too increasing, as we delve deeper into twenty-first century. Within six years, there may be so many of floods in a single year that they will totally shut down the world's lifeline 'food production'. In addition, the costs associated with these floods have become extensive both in lives and dollars. The countries of the world have to keep pouring out money to pay for the damages caused by these floods. And as time progresses and without any relief, there will no government on Earth capable of overcoming the destruction caused by these natural disasters. Money typically used to aid the needy, will no longer be available, and the cost of food will eventually rise to the point, where only the rich will be able to eat. The poor on the other hand, will have to pay a day's wage to be fed, just as foretold in the Book of Revelation.

Droughts

From the woes of the seven trumpet blast to the woes of the seven plagues, and now the woes of the seven vials are being poured out on Earth; one catastrophe then another catastrophe. The Earth will become a desolate scar form of its former beauty, and it is not yet over. The lands used for growing hay, corn, wheat and seeds are suffering from extreme droughts. If the farmers are unable to grow their crops, due to too much water; they can't grow crops without it. Not only do people need grains for food, but they are essential for all forms of livestock to eat; cattle need corn, chickens need grain, pigs need grain and cereal, etc... If these ranchers cannot get feed for their animals, then the price of meat will go skyward. Droughts are current in East Asia, Australia, United States, Russia, portions of Eastern Africa, and in South America.

There are drought areas in China, which have been the worst in fifty years, with the land parched and the irrigation dams dried up; both the crops and livestock are dying. The drought crisis in Somalia is causing a food epidemic lasting twelve years. In August 2010, Russia reported that it is experiencing its worst drought in at least fifty years, causing wheat prices biggest jump since 1973. There are no signs of the drought easing, and it may threaten sowing plans for winter grains.

In December 30, 2010, it was reported that a severe prolonged drought in Argentina, Brazil and Uruguay are raising fears that harvests of corn, wheat and soybean will fall short of expectations. Thereby, adding further pressure on a global commodity market, already strained by Russian, Australian and Pakistani weather conditions.

Twelve years ago, the rain stopped falling in Southeast Australia and since 1950 the average temperature has climbed 1.6 degrees Fahrenheit. There has been so little rain falling that surface flows across the region's river valleys have been cut 40 percent. Over the past decade, there has been so little water left in the lower sections of the Murray-Darling river system; that for every four out of ten days, the river doesn't even have enough flow to reach its mouth in the Great Southern Ocean, south of Adelaide. The drought has caused a catastrophic failure in rice production.

The western and southern United States has also been hit with a drought over the past five years. The lack of rain has resulted in huge forest fires, and the cattle ranchers have been unable to feed their livestock, forcing them to reduce the size, or get rid of their herd.

Thus far there have been deluges of worldwide devastations caused by the elements during the twentieth and twenty-first centuries, however, this is only the beginning of the tragedies. It is not by chance that all weather patterns have become extreme in our lifetime; they have become the tools of God to remind us that He is in control and not us. Virgin Mary visionaries are referring to these current natural disasters as minor chastisements by God.

That being so, it should be a wakeup call for humanity to alter its' current lifestyle, or these mini-chastisements by God will worsen.

If we do not redirect our lives and convert, we can anticipate that extreme weather will destroy all of our food supply in the near future, and a year's wage wouldn't be sufficient enough to buy enough food to live on for a day. Things made of gold, silver, brass and wood will be worthless, for they cannot fill an empty stomach. Those who enjoyed the riches of the earth, while their brothers and sisters starved in many countries, will now feel their pain of hunger. God will raise the valleys and lower the mountains; translated, all things on earth will be made equal where no man is richer than the other and all men will suffer.

Chapter 10

A Flood of Knowledge in Our Time

It is written in the Old Testament that knowledge will be poured out into the world in the end times. From Daniel (12:4), *"But as for you, Daniel, conceal these words and seal up the book until the end of time; many will go back and forth,* and *knowledge will increase."* The total written knowledge in the world had been estimated to have doubled between the years 1450 and 1750, and it took another two hundred fifty years to double again between the years 1750 and 1900. However, between the years 1900 and 1950, human intellect doubled once more and then again from 1950 to 1975. Currently, it is believed to double every two and half years. By the year 2020, global information is predicted to double every 72 days. Knowledge is essential for Satan to take command of the Earth, and to lead the world into destruction. At first technology and knowledge may appear as an angel of light, in that much of it was invented for good and peaceful purposes. After a while though, it will be misused and manipulated by those under demonic influence.

A whole new age of technology seemed to have sprung out of nowhere, beginning in the 1970s. In the healthcare sector, magnetic resonance imaging (MRI) enabled doctors to visualize the detailed internal human anatomy; thereby making it useful for imaging the brain, muscles, the heart, and cancers. There are other medical imaging machines; such as, ultrasound, MRI machines, PET and CT scanners, and x-ray machines. All of them aid doctors to diagnose problems inside patients without having to cut them open. There is a Gamma Knife, which is being used to treat brain tumors, by administering high-intensity radiation therapy in a small concentrated area. Other light-emitting devices use specific wavelengths of light to treat cancers. Heart transplants and arterial stints have become common and provide extended lifespans to people with heart disease. New drugs cure infections, treat cancer, cure diseases, etc.

All of these modern man-derived miracles have enabled patients to be given prolonged lives, but at what price? God has given us a certain amount of time on this Earth to fight against Satan and if we lose our way, will these new developments provide us enough time to find our way back? Even with advance medicines, each person has been given only so many days of life. Some may say that by having drawn-out lives, we could be doing more good works. However, we may be unnecessarily delaying the inevitable. In general, most people don't change when given a few extra years or even decades' of existence; they remain the same whether they are good or bad. Those who are evil will remain so, and Satan will continually use these servants to promote his wickedness and to further extend his reign on Earth.

In the 2000's, it seems that God even taught mankind the secrets of life itself with stem cell research, which is now being performed throughout the western cultures. With these former mysteries revealed, mankind can claim to be like god; after all, with cloning we can make a cloned sheep just from its DNA strains, and soon after, why not people? And if you need a new internal organ, it can be grown by using stem cells. God was no longer needed; he was just an antiquated belief for the ignorant masses.

There are those in the medical field who are talking of extending life spans into thousands of years, and who could afford it, except the rich? Some of the rich have obtained their money through illegal, corrupt and immoral ways, and if they could extend their lives, how many more ungodly acts would they commit? How many more innocent lives could they shatter? A short extension to a life would not be bad, if converted to do God's will. However, how many people have been given extended lives, and afterwards sought God to give Him thanks and to ask forgiveness for their sins? Imagine if the rich lived for a thousand years, how much hardened would they be, since they would have an era of invincibility.

The 1990s saw innovation unlike anything seen before with the electronic age. This age brought in the personal computer, cell phones, worldwide web CD's, DVD's, robots, GPS, video cameras, spy satellites with super sensitive spyware, electronic games, etc.

It was as if God poured out all kinds of hidden awareness upon mankind. The invention of personal computers, followed by "The International Web", provided the world with an infinite amount of data. As good as it sounds; that is, to grow intellectually by instantly sharing information by this means of communication, it would soon be abused by thieves and terrorist alike. All of these super sophisticated electronic advances have come with a cost. This loss of privacy can be seen with the extended numbers of cameras on top of buildings, on street poles, and on satellites. Cellular phones could be carried on one's person, and if they needed to be reached, all one had to do is call them; no longer was there a sense of having privacy.

Soon the government may require all citizens to wear under their skin an electronic identification badge. They will say that it for one's safety, so that your children or elderly parents can be tracked by GPS satellites in the event that someone takes them, or in case they get lost. Modern governments have the capability to track individuals by the GPS locater in their high tech smart-phones, and the individual doesn't even have to make a call to be tracked.

At the time of the antichrist, he will require every means of technology to prevent those from opposing him. He will use spy satellites, capable of taking a picture of a car's license plate from one hundred miles above the Earth, thereby tracking movements of people throughout the planet. He will also convince the public that high-tech spying systems are necessary to prevent terrorist from entering the country. This worldwide government, led by the antichrist, would use this vast data base to maintain power and control over the people.

During the time of the antichrist; everyone will have to accept his number to buy or sell anything. It would not be much different than it is today; most people have ATM cards, which can additionally be used to trace the whereabouts of an individual every time they take money out of the machine. In fact, ATM machines are capable of taking pictures of the individual withdrawing money. If someone opposes the antichrist, they wouldn't be able to get money out of their account, or if they were allowed to, it would be so that the authorities could find them. No buying or selling without the mark of the devil.

The Internet would be another ideal way for the antichrist to manipulate people. In 2011, Egypt's uprising and riots were accomplished with the aid of the International Web, used by the protestors to rise up against the government. The antichrist could get on the International Web or television and manipulate people, by promising them that he will stop any wars, economic discrepancies and food shortages. He will further declare that all will bode well for those who follow him. He will be very charismatic, much like Adolph Hitler, and the masses of people who are suffering and tired of war, will follow him.

This flood of knowledge upon mankind was exactly what Satan needs to bring his plans to fruition upon the Earth. Through the antichrist, he will be cunning and make people believe that they are making the right choices. People under the direction of the antichrist will misuse this intellectual base for Satan's personal gain. As time passes, medical advances could be used to threaten anyone or a loved one wishing to live longer. People will be given a choice, either live longer and worship him, or die.

Video games will manipulate people to become less compassionate; they will think there is no difference between killing a real person and killing a fictional bad guy on the video game. Satan will and does have people use cellular phone to explode IEDs (improvised explosive device) on groups of unsuspecting victims. Those aligned with Satan will utilize the Internet as a means to disclose information; such as, bomb making instructions, to spread false rumors, and to insight riots. All of this technology can be used by the antichrist to eavesdrop on our every spoken word that we say on the cellular phone; this way he can gather information about us.

The twentieth century is a very sweet one, filled with all the knowledge that was prophesized millenniums ago, by Daniel and as evidence that we are approaching the waning moments of Earth's history. These implements will become necessary to bring the world into a final climatic war. Satan has chosen this era; he has acquired the tools, and has gathered subservient individuals, who have given their allegiance to him. He is in the mood for a conflict that pits a war of technology against the power of God.

Chapter 11

The Beginning to the End

In the Book of Joel (4:1–2) it is written, "*He will bring his people back to Jerusalem, and that the nations of the world would be brought to the valley of Jehoshaphat where he will judge them because they had scattered his people throughout the world.*" This resettlement of Israel is the building block for the end times to begin. In Deuteronomy (30:3) it is written, "*then the LORD your God will restore your fortunes and have compassion on you, and he will gather you again from all the peoples where the LORD your God has scattered you*", or from Ezekiel (34:11–13), "For thus says the Lord GOD: *Behold, I, I myself will search for my sheep and will seek them out. As a shepherd seeks out his flock when he is among his sheep that have been scattered, so will I seek out my sheep, and I will rescue them from all places where they have been scattered on a day of clouds and thick darkness. And I will bring them out from the peoples and gather them from the countries, and will bring them into their own land. And I will feed them on the mountains of Israel, by the ravines, and in all the inhabited places of the country.*"

What makes these prophetic gatherings of God's chosen ones so significant is that the Book of Revelation declared that the Jewish nation will exists; in fact, not only will it exists, but its' enemies will be at its doorstep. At the end of time, an army consisting of 200 million soldiers will stand against Israel. For over two thousand years; after the destruction and exile of the Jews from Israel, the Jewish people had been scattered throughout the world. However, not only is there an Israeli State once more, but there are also seven billion people on the planet; more than capable of generating the army of 200 million soldiers spoken of in the Book of Revelation.

Prior to the twentieth century it would have been a hopeless attempt for the Jews to try to establish a Jewish nation in the lands of their forefathers. They were a despised people dispersed across the world, and had no adequate means to establish an army and retake the land of their ancestors. They would have been hopelessly outnumbered by the Arabs, and any attempt to return to their homeland would have ended in failure. However, the concept of establishing a Jewish state was not unheard of. It was initiated in the Balfour Declaration of 1917, a British government policy, which supported the establishment of a Jewish homeland in Palestine. However, it fell short of becoming a reality.

Satan knows that the Jewish people are the stumbling block for his conquest to reign over all human souls. A Jewish Israeli State represents that timeline written in the Book of Revelation, which clearly identifies the Jewish people living once more in Israel just prior to Jesus's return. Satan therefore devised a scheme to eliminate every Jewish person in the world. His reasoning may have been, if there are no Jews, then there would never be a Jewish state, and prophecy will not be fulfilled.

Ironically, it was evil that enable the Jewish people to come back to Israel. Adolf Hitler held the Jews responsible for the German peoples' suffering. He unified the country with anti-Semitic beliefs, and it was during World War II when Satan decided to eliminate the Jewish threat, by using the Nazi Germans as his pawns. It was called "The Final Solution", an idea conceived by Heinrich Himmler, who was Reichsführer of the Schutzstaffel (SS) unit in Nazi Germany. He detailed the systematic genocide of European Jews. However, it was none other than Adolf Hitler who approved this conception of Himmler's to eliminate the Jewish existence in the world. The result of the Nazi efforts was that they murdered; by means of gas poisoning (cyanide and carbon monoxide), shootings, starvations and cremation, approximately six million Jews before the conclusion of the war.

Satan's intention to eliminate the Jews through the hands of the Nazi's backfired. In fact there was so much empathy for the Jewish people, due to the holocaust, that on November 29, 1947 the United Nations General Assembly resolved to divide Palestine into three parts. In the exact wording of the resolution passed, "Independent Arab and Jewish States and the Special International

Regime for the City of Jerusalem ... shall come into existence in Palestine."

Less than half a year later, on May 14, 1948, David Ben-Gurion stood before the Provisional State Council in Tel Aviv and proclaimed the State of Israel. However, Satan had not conceded, and from May 14 to June 11, 1948, the Arab League members consisting of Egypt, Transjordan, Syria, Lebanon and Iraq refused to accept the UN partition plan, and instead proclaimed the right of self-determination for the Arabs across the whole of Palestine. A few months later, on October 1, 1948, Amin al-Husayni, the mufti of Jerusalem, stood before the Palestine National Council in Gaza and declared the existence of the All-Palestine State. In essence, he declared war on Israel, which initiated the first Arab-Israeli war that took place from 1948-49. The war was a victory for the Jewish army.

Satan wasn't going to give up easily, and there were four more attempts to destroy Israel by the Arabs. There was the 1956 Arab-Israeli war, the 1967 war against the Arabs, the Yon Kippur War in 1973-74 and the 1982 war. The Six-Day War was fought from June 5-10, 1967 between Israel and the neighboring states of Egypt Jordan, and Syria. Prior to the war, there was a high degree of unrest between Israel and its neighbors, so on June 5, 1967 Israel launched surprise air strikes against Arab forces and the war began. The outcome was a swift and decisive Israeli victory, which gave them control of the Gaza Strip, the Golan Heights, the Sinai Peninsula, and both the West Bank and East Jerusalem. All of this land re-established an Israel state that was reminiscent of its old kingdom, prior to its destruction by the Roman legions in 73A.D.

If this were the opening of a Broadway play, it could be said that the stage is set (time), the props are in place (technologies and changes in human ideologies) and the characters (those who have accepted Satan) are defined for the opening act for the decisive battle. The war of Armageddon will take place only if Israel remains a state. Therefore Israel has become the key sign that the return of Jesus is not far off. One more key fact from the Book of Revelation (9:16), *"The number of cavalry troops was two hundred million; I heard their number..."*

Chapter 12

Seers

The bible has always had prophetic warnings of futuristic times when God was about ready to punish mankind. The first warning was when He had Noah build the ark, as described in the Book of Genesis (Chapters 6, 7). God saw how wicked and depraved mankind had become, so He decided to rid the Earth of human beings, by means of a flood. All of mankind, with the exception of Noah and his family, would be eliminated by a deluge of water. God instructed Noah how to build the ark, and for him to collect and place on the ark, every type of male and female animal. The dimensions of the ark were 450 feet long, 75 feet wide and 45 feet high. It took Noah about 120 years to build the ark, and he was 600 yrs. old by the time he completed this task.

One can imagine the humiliation and ridicule that Noah suffered day after day from the people of Nephilim, the city where Noah lived and built the ark. Every time it rained, poor Noah would have probably been laughed at by the people, who were saying "run ever body, the flood is coming, the flood is coming". It took great faith by Noah to continue his objective under these conditions for such long period of a time. Ironically, this same amount of time was equally given to people to change from their evil ways, obviously to no avail. The floods did come as predicted and all the people, with the exception of Noah and his family, being killed.

Another biblical account that God was going to punish the wicked people was written in the Old Testament Book of Jonah (Chapters 2, 3). God told Jonah that Nineveh, a large city requiring three days to traverse through, would be destroyed because of its' wickedness. Jonah was told by God to go through the city proclaiming, *"Forty days more and Nineveh shall be destroyed"*. Upon hearing this, the king declared that everyone should not eat, nor drink, wear sackcloth and turn from their evil ways. When God saw they had repented, He did not destroy the city. This is a case where God was going to destroy wickedness, but relented upon their conversion.

Just as it was for Noah, the people of Nineveh must have thought that Jonah was crazy walking up and down the streets yelling, "The end is near, the end is near." Poor Jonah, he must have felt terrible to have the burden of proclaiming death and destruction was going to come down from Heaven. However, when the city was not destroyed, the people would have said that it would never have been demolished anyway, and all they did was waste their time sacrificing for nothing. The world that we live in today is no different than those of Noah and Jonah's time. There are selected individuals walking up and down the streets carrying signs predicting the end is near, and most people believe that these self-proclaimed prophets are nuts. They are not about to listen to these prophets, or change their ways; for them it would be a waste of time. Are today's critics any different than those of Noah's days?

In Genesis (Chapter 18), God had foretold Abraham that the wickedness in the cities of Sodom and Gomorrah were so great that He was going to destroy them with fire and brimstone. Abraham negotiated with God not to destroy them, if he could find only ten righteous people in the city. Unfortunately for the peoples of Sodom and Gomorrah, he could not find ten righteous people and both cities were reduced to ashes.

God always forewarns us of upcoming calamities. He gives us enough time to prepare ourselves through conversion, but time after time we ignore Him and go on living the same way that we did. However, God's patience does grow thin and in His timeframe, He will fulfill His promise. God has always used prophets to give humanity foreknowledge of future events. The greater magnitude of the event, the more time God gives us to prepare for it; such as in Isaiah (7:14), *"Therefore the Lord himself will give you a sign, the virgin will be with child and will give birth to a son, and will call him Immanuel."* This was a prediction of Jesus's birth, 750 years beforehand. It was a major episode in humanity, in which generation after generation of Jews had waited for the birth of their Messiah. However, when Jesus was finally born, they didn't believe it. After all, it is the typical philosophy of "not in in my lifetime, it must be in somebody else's." Their expectations were the Messiah was to be born from someone with a more aristocratic bloodline. They had waited so long for their Messiah; they couldn't accept that poor and humble people like Joseph and Mary would be chosen by God to give birth to their Messiah. Their King!

God keeps His promise, and for over two thousand years He has been preparing us for the end of our world. He has warned us in the Old and New Testaments of the Bible, and He has warned us through the prophets and even civilizations throughout time. Something as serious as destroying the Earth, God is not going to yell out at the last minute and say, "ready or not here I come". He will give us ample time to convert, and as the event draws closer, He will use every means to save as many people as possible. The problem remains for us is to accept the messages given by modern day prophets and respond to them like the wise king of Nineveh, who can be credited in saving his city.

The difficulty remains how do we decipher between the real and the false prophets? Even Jesus warned us of false prophets (Matthew 7:15-16), *"Beware of false prophets, who come to you in sheep's clothing, but underneath are ravenous wolves. By their fruits you will know them."* Jesus points at the fruits of their works; in other words, what do people gain by saying they come in the name of God and are acting as His messengers. God wants to save us all from damnation. If there are messengers of God saying the world is going to be destroyed, we should determine whether the true fruit of their work is for monetary profit. In contrast, there are honest and humble messengers warning us to convert, and they have received no monetary gain, or seek fame for themselves. The true prophets actually prefer to remain hidden from notoriety, but feel compelled to do His will. These individuals are more likely to be from God.

There have been many prophets who have begun warning humanity about the end times even before the death of Jesus. After Jesus's death, several noteworthy individuals and old civilizations have warned us, that the twentieth and twenty-first centuries would be a period of great upheaval. There have been false prophets, who claimed the end of the world would be in the year 666, others in 1000 and yet others in 2000. They were no basis for their prophecies other than dates. There have been hundreds if not thousands end world predictions. These false prophets are the ones who have caused people to scoff at the true gift of prophecy. For nonbelievers, their mindsets have been hardened due to these charlatans, and their thought then becomes, "Since it hasn't happened yet, it never will." In reality, the gift of prophecy is a rare one; given out to selected individuals by the Holy Spirit. In Romans (12:6) Paul writes, "*Since we have gifts that differ according to the grace given to us, let us exercise them: if prophecy, in proportion to faith*".

It must also be remembered Satan will also have his deceivers making prophecies; by him doing this, he spreads confusion and at the same time discredits those having the true gift of prophecy. He will have so many of these frauds prophesizing the end times are coming that many people will stop believing it will ever happen; in this manner leaving only a few individuals capable of recognizing the true prophets. It is important that we decipher the messages of these true prophets 'visionaries', and avoid listening to people predicting the world will end on an 'exact hour and date'. At the same moment, it is equally important to understand, we are living in a season of evilness.

We should be aware that further acts of disobedience cannot continue without repercussions from God. It doesn't take the gift of prophecy to see the world is currently in turmoil. Wars, instability, loss of faith, worldwide economic collapse, social and moral decay, disintegration of ethical values, etc. have all been discussed. Therefore we should carefully consider the words and warnings coming from these prophetic individuals, some of whom saw times such as these unfolding many years ago, while others are predicting God's chastisements are about to befall us in the near future.

There have been notable prophets, who saw into the future and described images they could not comprehend. Some saw inventions that were far beyond their understanding. Nevertheless, they wrote down what they envisioned to the best of their ability.

Boiling Point 2017

Some of these prophets include Mother Shipton, Nostradamus, and a modern day visionary named Edgar Cayce.

Mother Shipton lived from 1488-1561 and was an English soothsayer, whose prophecies were first appeared in print in the year 1641, eighty years after her death. Like Nostradamus, her prophecies are written in rhythmic stanzas, but they do not need interpretations, as do Nostradamus' stanzas. As shown in the following written stanzas, it could be interpreted that she may have accurately seen the internet, phone, steel ships, cars, diving suits, jets, television, and submarines more than four hundred years before her death.

(Internet, phone)

Around the world men's thoughts will fly
Quick as the twinkling of an eye.
And water shall great wonders do
How strange. And yet it shall come true.

(Steel ships and America)

In water, iron, then shall float, as easy as a wooden boat, Gold shall be seen in stream and stone in land that is yet unknown.

(Cars and, diving suits, subs and airplanes)

Through towering hills proud men shall ride, No horse or ass move by his side. Beneath the water, men shall walk shall ride, shall sleep, shall even talk. And in the air men shall be seen in white and black and even green.

(Television, submarines and planes)

When pictures seem alive with movements free, when boats like fishes swim beneath the sea, when men like birds shall scour the sky; then half the world, deep drenched in blood shall die.

Many people may deny her gift of prophecy and would say that her stanzas could be interpreted to mean other things. However, given the era she lived in, it would be highly improbable for her to guess many of these inventions that we have today. Therefore, the Holy Spirit most probably gave her this gift to foresee the future. After all, John of Patmos was given the same gift of prophecy, but no one questioned his gift because he was a man living in a time when women were never given credit for any accomplishments. Consequently, it is necessary to accept that God can speak to anyone; man, woman, or child in order for His messages to be heard. God is not diminutive minded and think as men do. Thus it is important to heed her predictions of a more dire time, when evil has pervaded our world; filling men with greed and having them do ungodly works.

In some stanzas, she sees a world chastised by God, where only a few people are left on the face of the Earth, requiring mankind to start the human race again. This destruction by nature will cause men to tremble, and no nation or man can prevent it.

(End of time)
*And when the dragon's tail is gone,
man forgets,
and smiles, and carries on*
**To apply himself - too late, too late
For mankind has earned deserved fate.**

(Decimation of the world)
**For those who live the century through
in fear and trembling this shall do.**
Flee to the mountains and the dens to bog and forest and wild fens.

(Tribulation)
*And in some far off distant land
Some men - oh such a tiny band
Will have to leave their solid mount*
**And span the Earth, those few to count,
Who survives this will then begin the human race again.**

(Fallen mankind)
**And murder foul and brutal deed
when man will only think of greed.** *And man shall walk as if asleep He does not look - he many not peep.*

She foretells of a horrible war being plotted by deceitful men; perhaps this war will be World War III. There is also a warning, in an unknown land to her, of a great upheaval upon Earth when volcanoes erupt and cover cities under mud; following them are earthquakes that destroy cities. Her reference of lands as yet known to me and three sleeping mountains may refer to America's Yellowstone National Park, which contains a super volcano, which is actually a volcanic field where the latest three super volcanoes erupted simultaneously 640,000 years ago, and are due to erupt again.

(Wars)
The kings shall false promise make
and talk just for talking's sake.
And nations plan horrific war.
And taxes rise and lively down as
nations wear perpetual frown.

(Volcanic Eruptions)
Yet greater sign be there to see.
The like as never seen before
As man nears latter century
Three sleeping mountains gather
breath
And spew out mud, and ice and
death.
And earthquakes swallow town and town,
in lands as yet to me unknown

She describes a period of several days and nights when some form of catastrophic event will cause the ocean waters rise to unheard of levels. This rise in the height of the water resembles what tsunamis do after an underwater volcanic eruption, or when there is under water continental slip between the plates causing an earthquake, or a large meteor striking the ocean.

(Tsunamis)
For seven days and seven nights
Man will watch this awesome sight.
The tides will rise beyond their ken
to bite away the shores and then
the mountains will begin to roar
and earthquakes split the plain to shore.

Her depiction of the Angel Gabriel blowing his horn comes directly out of revelation; when the angels blow their trumpets and disaster after disaster come upon the Earth, in retribution for the sins of mankind. Afterwards, the old dead world will be replaced with a new world, much like that described in Revelation (Chapter 21:1), *"Then I saw a new heaven and new Earth. The former heaven and former Earth had passed away…"* The initial response of mankind due to these catastrophes will be to flee, yet even then, they will maintain their sinful ways of killing and raping. No remorse, no fear, just do as they please to do until the last moment.

For storms will rage and oceans roar When **Gabriel stands on sea and shore** *and as he blows his wondrous horn Old worlds die and new ones will be born.*	***Man flees in terror from the floods*** *and kills, and rapes and lies in blood and spilling blood by mankind's hands will stain and bitter many land.*

    Other individuals who had the gift of prophecy include the world's most renowned seer, Michel de Nostradamus, who lived from 1503-1566. He was well known for his gift of seeing futuristic events. One of his more famous predictions was in Quatrain C1-35, "*The young lion will overcome the old one on the field of battle in single combat: He will put out his eyes in a cage of gold: Two fleets one, then to die a cruel death.*" Nostradamus accurately predicted that King Henry II of France would be killed in a jousting match; after an opponent's lance breaks into splinters, and enters into the king's eyes. The jousting match did take place and the opponents lance did break into pieces. It was found that both splinters had penetrated the king's brain, and it required several days before the king died (*to die a cruel death*).

    Another prediction by Nostradamus pertains to the legacy of Napoleon Bonaparte, whom Nostradamus believed to be one of the three antichrists that would come upon the Earth. In Quatrains C1.60 and C8.57, Nostradamus predicted exactly where Napoleon would be born, and he would rise to power through the military, rather than being a born child of royalty. In actuality, Napoleon was born on Corsica, an island in the Mediterranean ocean next to Italy, and he was a second lieutenant in the French Army, but after the French Revolution he became Emperor of France (*from short robe he will attain the long robe*). Napoleon was a viscous conqueror, but was severely defeated by the Russians, and it cost his country dearly through lives lost, hence, "*He shall be found less a Prince than a butcher.*"

Quatrain C1.60
An Emperor shall be born near Italy
Who shall cost the Empire dear,
They shall say, with what people he keeps company.
He shall be found less a Prince than a butcher.

Quatrain C8: 57
From a simple soldier he will rise to the empire,
From the short robe he will attain the long.

Nostradamus ability to accurately predict the future did not stop with Napoleon, he also accurately predicted in Quatrain C2.24 that Adolf Hitler, would be the Chancellor of Germany during World War II, and would be defeated by the allied forces, *"Beasts wild with hunger will cross the rivers. The greater part of the battlefield will be against Hister. In armor steel they will make their great assault."* Hister is an anagram for Hitler and the "Beasts wild with hunger will cross the rivers" may refer to the allied troops crossing the rivers into Germany, spear headed by General Patton's tanks (*armor steel*).

Every prophet must have predictions that substantiate their ability to see into the future. These predictions by Nostradamus legitimized him as an individual, who truly had this gift; therefore, his other predictions should be taken seriously. Nostradamus made multiple prophecies regarding the twentieth and twenty-first centuries; such as, a Christian-Muslin War, World War III, a large asteroid or comet hitting the Earth, great famine, and the end of an age.

There are those who believe that a Christian-Muslin war will precipitate the beginning for the end of the world and in Quatrain C5.68 Nostradamus makes reference to camels' drinking water from the river Danube, which can be interpreted as the presence of Muslims in Europe; a prelude and requirement for a Christian-Muslin War.

Quatrain C5.68
***In the Danube and the Rhine will come to drink
the great Camel, not repenting it:***
*The Rhone to tremble, much stronger than the Loire
and near the Alps the Cock will ruin him.*

Camels drinking from the Danube and the Rhine rivers, both located in Germany, would appear to be ludicrous at the time of Nostradamus. However, Arab or Muslim people (nomadic people) are often associated with camels, and this quatrain indicates that there will be a significant number of Muslims in Europe, especially in Germany. At the time of Nostradamus, a small number of Muslims were living in limited areas of Europe, but Christians dominated the region of France, Germany, Italy, Austria, etc. Currently, the Muslim population has spread throughout all of Europe, propagated by a large influx of immigrants. In 2005, 85% of Europe's total population growth was attributed to immigration, and currently 7% of Europe's immigration population equate to 49 million Muslims. The Muslim population in Europe has doubled since 1979 and by the year 2015, it is expected to double again, so now the probability of a war has become more realistic; especially, if sleeper cells (terrorist) are present in great numbers.

What could initiate a Christian-Muslim war? The presence of western powers in the Middle East has stirred up old but not forgotten hatred towards 'the infidels'. When life is difficult it is easy to find someone to attribute for your suffering and many of Muslim people are blaming the West for their decrepit lives. They believe the West is responsible for either taking away all of their countries' resources (oil), or for keeping their hated leader in power.

Some of the extreme religious groups believe that Islam is the only true religion; they accuse the West of suppressing European-Muslims from practicing their religion. These extremist are utilizing suffering, religious persecution and subjugation by the government as tools to recruit their 'down-trodden' brethren throughout the world to join their cause. In the event these extremist should persuade the majority of Muslim people to start a war against the western culture; they can easily organize terror networks throughout Europe, having already have established a significant presence.

One of Nostradamus's most intriguing futuristic predictions about the end of time is about a great slaughter taking place near the beginning of the new millennium when "the seventh number is accomplished".

Quatrain C10.74
The year the great seventh number is accomplished,
Appearing at the time of the great games of slaughter:
Not far from the age of the great millennium,
When the dead will come out of their graves

The use of the word 'slaughter' could be interpreted, as the time when billions of people will be dying, which comes to fulfillment during the tribulation. The *'seventh number is accomplished'* could be a reference within Revelation (11:15–16) when the **seventh trumpet is blown** and the voices in heaven proclaim "*the* **world now belongs** *to our Lord and his Anointed and he will reign forever and ever*". The seventh trumpet being *'the great seventh number'* and the words *'year and accomplished'* portraying that the world is now God's and Satan has been defeated.

Another possibility for the first line of this quatrain also comes from the Book of Revelation (16: 17–21) when the seventh bowl was poured out upon the Earth, "*And* **the seventh** *angel poured out his bowl into the air, a loud voice came out of the temple from the throne saying* **"it is done…"** *And there were voices, and thunders, and lightnings; and there was a great earthquake, such as was not since men were upon the Earth, so mighty an earthquake, and so great…And the great city was divided into three parts, and the cities of the nation's fell: and great Babylon came in remembrance before God, to give unto her the cup of the wine of the fierceness of His wrath… And every island fled away, and the mountains were not found… And there fell upon men a great hail out of heaven, every stone about the weight of a talent: and men blasphemed God because of the plague of the hail; for the plague thereof was exceeding great."*

Another interpretation of the 'seventh number being accomplished' could even refer to a year containing the number seven. Nostradamus indicates that these things are accomplished just into the new millennium, and the number seven could represent the years 2007, 2017 or even 2027. Only the years 2017 and 2027 are feasible candidates for this representation of the number seven. It was previously written, God granted Satan one hundred years to try to destroy his church. If God gave Satan one hundred years, it is only logical that he would send someone to help humanity, and other than His Son, the Virgin Mary would be His choice. If Mary's appearance at Fatima in 1917 roughly equated to the beginning of Satan's timeframe, then Satan's one hundred years would end in the same year as Mary's, that being in 2017. Therefore this could be the interpretation of Nostradamus's quatrain, *'The year (2017) the great seventh number is accomplished'*, is the year when Satan's time is up.

Clearly Nostradamus is referring to a time shortly after the year 2000, with these apocalyptic warnings. He doesn't stop there, for he also writes about a time of distress in the world. In Quatrains C1.67 and C6.5 he warns of a worldwide famine. And currently, after many decades of abundant crops, the world is experiencing food shortages and food prices are beginning to spiral out of control. Climate changes have contributed to these shortages, and it is anticipated that these shortages will worsen. Africa has suffered the worst of the shortages, and in Somalia alone it is estimated that hundreds of thousands of people may die. This may be the onset of what Nostradamus foresees as worldwide starvation; closely matching that written in the Book of Revelation describing the rider on a black horse. This rider representing a time in our world when there will be immense food shortages and widespread hunger.

Quatrain C1.67
The great famine which I sense approaching
Will often turn [up in various areas] then become worldwide.
It will be so vast and long-lasting that [people] will grab
Roots from the trees and children from the breast.

Quatrain C6.5
So great a famine due to uncontrollable weather
through incessant rain from an expanding arctic pole,
Pouring in a hundred places in the (northern) hemisphere,
when they shall live without laws or government.

Boiling Point 2017

In quatrain C6.5 Nostradamus is predicting the melting of the artic poles, and when this happens; currently they are actually are experiencing unprecedented melting, there will be devastating weather patterns that will flood many parts of the world. Another of his prophecies specifies that the world will experience conditions of extreme famine at the turn of the millennium. This can be found in Quatrain C2.46, when he writes "the great cycle of the centuries is renewed" there will be famine in the land, along with wars and during that time, a comet will appear. This comet 'great star' mentioned in Quatrain C2.41 will be so close to the Earth that it will look to be the size of the sun. The Book of Revelation (9:1) also makes mention of objects falling from the sky that will bring distress upon the world "The *fifth angel blew his trumpet and a star had fallen from the sky to the Earth"*. Can these two be related and Nostradamus was writing of this end time?

Quatrain C2:46
After great misery for mankind an even greater one approaches, when the **great cycle of the centuries is renewed. It will rain blood, milk, famine, war and disease. In the sky will be seen a fire, dragging a tail of sparks.**

Quatrain C2.41
The great star *for seven days will burn,*
The cloud will cause two suns to appear:
The big mastiff all night will howl,
When **the great pontiff changes countries**

The last line in Quatrain C2.41 refers to the pope changing countries. Apparently this comet signals the beginning for imminent destruction throughout the world, which has also been foretold by current twentieth century visionaries, who have been seeing the Blessed Virgin Mary. Is it possible that this comet will cause the city of Rome to be destroyed, and that the pope will have to leave it? This corroborates directly with Fatima's third secret, in which Lucia, one of the Virgin Mary visionaries, saw a vision of the pope going through a city in half-ruin.

The third line of Quatrain C2.41 makes reference to the 'big mastiff' howling all night. The mastiff dog was bred in England and used as a watchdog for *more than two thousand years*. The use of the word mastiff in this quatrain may be symbolic of watching for the return of Jesus (*more than two thousand years*), which could come to fruition upon the arrival of this comet.

Nostradamus further predicts when a comet called the NIBIRU hits the Earth; nearly the whole of Asia will be flooded by a monstrous Tsunami. The comet will cause the Earth to lose its orbit around the sun and that there will be massive Earthquakes. Nostradamus prediction of the world losing its orbit around the sun, followed by many earthquakes, corroborates with other cultures that predict this same finality of Earth. One such culture is the ancient Mayans.

Chapter 13

Prophecy

The Mayan's were masters in studying the universe and its' movements. They believed the Earth goes through cycles of life; when the old is destroyed, a new one is formed. This follows closely with Revelation (21: 1), in which the world is destroyed, and a new Heaven and new Earth are formed. The Mayan's very accurate astronomical observations determined the end of the world will be on December 12, 2012. This is when all the planets in our solar system align themselves in a straight line towards the center of the Milky Way Galaxy.

The Mayans predicted that at the start of the planets alignment, disasters will befall the planet. According to the Mayans, the Earth had been destroyed five times before. The alignment of the planets may have an unprecedented gravitational effect upon the Earth. This gravitational effect may either cause the magnetic poles to change, or flip the Earth on its precessional axis. There is scientific evidence suggesting the Earth flips on its precessional axis every 26,000 years. It is also known the North and South poles have switched before more than once. In Hindu texts these cycles are called Yugas.

For the people upon the planet, the effect of the Earth flipping on its precessional axis would have the appearance described in Revelation (6:12–14), *"Then the stars of the sky fell to the Earth like green figs falling from trees shaken by mighty winds. And the sky was rolled up like a scroll and taken away"*. Another reference to the Earth possibly flipping on its axis, comes out of the Book of Isaiah (24:1), *"Behold, the Lord makes the Earth empty, and makes it waste, and turns it upside down."*

Recently scientists have been investigating the possibility of the Earth's magnetic poles reversing, *Nature, 435* (7043). They have determined by analyzing the intensity and strength of magnetization in the rocks, as one goes down through the sedimentary layers that every switch in polarity results at the moment, when the field is at its weakest. Currently, the Earth's magnetic field has been decreasing and is reaching a low point. This geomagnetic reversal or 'polar reversal' results in the Earth's magnetic field changing its' magnetic north to become magnetic south and vice versa. Prior to this change, when the magnetic fields have depreciated to minuscule levels, or as the 'trekkies' would refer to it as 'the deflection shield is down', we could be susceptible to significant solar damage

Could the alignment of the planets cause the poles to switch? If they do, will the Earth be vulnerable to the sun's solar flares, which are supposed to be at, or near, maximum activity at that time? Could this planetary alignment cause the Earth to flip on its precessional axis through some sort of gravitational effect? If the Earth flips instantaneously on its axis, the world would experience devastating tsunamis, earthquakes and even volcanic activity; the likes not seen throughout all human history.

These predictions by Nostradamus coincide with a modern day seer named Edgar Cayce. Edgar Cayce is the most famous psychic of the 20th century and probably one of the most famous ever. He gave over 14,000 readings while in a trance state. Edgar Cayce accurately predicted in 1924 that the stock market would crash in 1929. Cayce predicted that India would become independent from Britain; fulfilled in 1947, at which time India began a transition to a democratic republic. In 1938, Cayce correctly described the location of an Essene community, which was discovered when the Dead Sea Scrolls were found in 1948. In 1932, Cayce advised the Jews to regard the advent of Fascist anti-Semitism in Europe as the time to fulfill the biblical prophecy, which foretold that the Jews would return to Israel.

Futuristic predictions by Edgar Cayce include, *"that there will be upheavals in the Arctic and Antarctic that will cause the eruption of volcanoes in the torrid areas, and pole shift"*, and *"The greater portion of Europe will be changed in the twinkling of an eye."* Cayce predicted sometime between the years 1958 and 1998, the Earth's surface will begin to change, *"Where there has been a frigid or semi-tropical climate, there will be a more tropical one, and moss and fern will grow."* Currently Greenland that was covered in ice has lost a major amount of its glaciers cover and is becoming green. The cause for these dramatic climatic changes will be the result of the Earth shifting its magnetic poles around the year 2000. Currently, scientists are predicting a magnetic pole reversal may soon take place. Cayce's reference to Europe changing in a twinkling of an eye could be the result of Earths' flipping on its axis. This would cause countries to be located at different latitudes, and could resemble the same appearance on the Earth that was written in the Book of Revelation (8:12), *"When the fourth angel blew his trumpet, a third of the sun, a third of the moon and a third of the stars were struck, so that a third of them became dark."*

Cayce believed humanity would soon experience a day of reckoning, and he predicted the year of the Second Coming of Jesus to be 1998. His other prophecies for the Jesus's Second Coming are, *"His messenger shall appear there"*, *"for the time and times and half times are at an end"* and *"The sun will be darkened and there shall be proclaimed through the spiritual interception in the hearts and minds and souls that his star has appeared and will point the way for those who enter into the Holy of Holies in themselves. He will appear!"*

Although his date of Jesus' return is obviously wrong, Marian visionaries have often said that some of God's chastisements have been delayed or avoided, so although Edgar Cayce's prediction for the Second Coming of Jesus Christ is wrong, it is still within the approximate season.

A related but an entirely different perspective on the Second Coming of Jesus comes from a woman, who attempted suicide in 1991 and had a near death experience. During her deathlike state, she met the Lord and was provided with an understanding about suffering in this world. Prior to her coming back to life, she saw the urgency in the angels, who were scurrying about to do the work of God. She was told that we are in the final moments before the Savior returns to the Earth, and the war between darkness and light upon the Earth had grown intense. She was told that if we are not continually seeking light, the darkness will consume us, and we will lose our souls. She understood that the Earth was being prepared for the Second Coming of

Jesus, although she was not aware of the time of his return. Her projected timeline of Jesus's return coincides with Nostradamus and Edgar Cayce predictions.

Throughout history there have been other civilizations predicting the end of time. It is interesting that each civilization has independently chosen the twentieth or early twenty-first century as the time. The Mayan civilization based their end time scenario to be in the year 2012, when their god, Quetzalcoatl, returns. Quetzalcoatl is the god of intelligence and self-reflection, a patron of priests. One can speculate that Quetzalcoatl mirrors Jesus in that he has knowledge, love and is a priest.

Another Indian tribe, the Hopi Indians of the American West predicted, prior to the settlement of white people in North American, white people would inhabit their land carrying thunder sticks (guns), and would travel by means of a spinning wheel (covered wagons). They spoke of the land being crossed by snakes of iron (railroad), and the land being crossed by a spider's web (telegraph wires). They spoke of the sea turning black (oil spills?) causing many living things to die. They prophesized when you will hear of a dwelling place in the heavens, above the Earth, that shall fall with a great crash. It will appear as a blue star.

According to them, humanity is in its fifth world, just as the Mayans have documented. The Hopi's predict that after the year 2012, humanity will have a choice between peace and harmony, or it will go through a time of suffering and purification before the time of 'one-heartedness' comes about. One-heartedness could infer the Lord Jesus Christ, who is all consumed with love and this represents his return.

The American Cherokee Indians had their apocalyptic version as well. Their prophecies are relatively new, compared to the Mayan prophecies. Theirs were made in the early 1800s by the members of their tribe. The Cherokee Indians predicted their feathered serpent god was going to return in 2012. The Cherokee peoples believe the Earth will undergo three shakings before the end times. The first shaking was believed to be the onset of World War I, and the second shaking was the advent of World War II. The third shaking will be much more destructive and will start after men have learned to build a house in the sky. The house in the sky could be the International Space Station. When this house in the sky is built, we are warned that we will know the Great Spirit is about to grab the Earth, this time not with one hand, but with both hands.

Across the world, the Hindus' Lord Krishna tells Ganga Devi that a Golden Age will come in the Kali Yuga, referring to one of the four ages the world goes through as part of the cycle of eras. Lord Krishna predicted this Golden Age will start 5,000 years after the beginning of the Kali Yuga, and it will last for 10,000 years. This shift of Ages is expected to come in this century, and coincides with a new world emerging at the same time of the Mayan's date in December 2012 AD. The cause for this change is from human beings: spiritual darkness (loss of faith), violence, lies, hypocrisy, intelligence, ignorance, ruthlessness, cruelty, greed, laziness, corruption, destruction, loss of morals, lack of self-discipline, abusiveness, etc. This list resembles very much the same reasons that Paul, the Apostle had written in the letter to Timothy when he referred to the end times.

Other ancient warnings of catastrophic times upon the Earth were written by an oracle known as Sybil, who lived during the time of the ancient Greeks. She lived in a cave and wrote down her visions; some included Alexander the Great's conquest of the known world and the birth of Jesus. One of her predictions was directed toward our own time *"These things in the tenth generation shall come to pass. The Earth shall be shaken by a great earthquake that throws many cities into the sea. There shall be war. Fire shall come flashing down from the heavens and many cities will burn. Black ashes shall fill the great sky. Then know the anger of the Gods."*

This massive earthquake that she depicted, could be the same one written in the Book of Revelation (6:12), *"Then I watched while he broke opened the sixth seal, and there was a great earthquake, the sun turned black as sackcloth."* In both predictions, there is a massive earthquake and the sky is filled with ashes, so much so, the sun's light is blocked out. In the passage from revelation, the earthquake is the wrath of God and in her prophecy; she writes that people will know the anger of God.

A different type of prophecy was from St. Malachi, who in the year 1139, made up a list of 112 short phrases in Latin to describe each of the Roman Catholic Popes. The list began with Pope Celestine II, who was elected pope in 1143 and it goes through our current pope. He predicted that Pope John Paul I would be elected and short-lived. He described him as of the half of the moon. Pope John Paul I was elected on the half moon, and died one month later on the half moon. Next he predicted Pope John Paul II as being of the eclipse of the sun, or from the labor of the sun. And because of his devotion to Virgin Mary, Pope John Paul II might also be seen to be the fruit of the intercession of the Woman Clothed with the Sun in labor (Revelation 12:1–2). His funeral was on April 8, 2005 when there was a solar eclipse visible in the Americas.

The last true pope on St Malachi's list, before the hardships begin, was described as one being of *Gloria olivæ*, which could refer to our current Pope Benedict XVI. Gloria Olivae is a branch of the Benedictine Order and since Pope Benedict is affiliated with this order, he could be the one filling this prophecy. However, there is some debate whether someone described as Peter, will be after Gloria Olivae. This pope shall be seated during the end times and St Malachi's' prediction for him is, "In extreme persecution, the seat of the Holy Roman Church will be occupied by Peter the Roman, who will feed the sheep through many tribulations, at the term of which the *city of seven hills will be destroyed* and the formidable Judge will judge his people." The formable Judge apparently is in reference to God at the end times. Interestingly, if Peter is the last pope, it correlates with the concept of symmetry, as previously discussed in Chapter 3; such that, the church began with Peter and ends with Peter.

All of these prophecies by individuals and civilizations are proof that God has been warning humanity of it ultimate demise long before it will become a reality. The prophets' warnings were resolute that the reason for civilizations' destruction was due to their total disregard for the truth and the rejection of God. God did not wait until the only the twentieth century to warn us, He has been telling us for hundreds of years about these times by having old men dream, dreams. He has pulled out all the stops for us to believe in Him and His wrath of judgment. Since many of these prophets have been ignored, He is now moving to another, more direct way to warn us. His choice happens to be by having the Virgin Mary's presence on Earth.

God must be saying, "Surely they will listen to the mother of My Son". He is sending her to guide us to repentance and to abstain from our ways of sin. Mary has appeared to many peoples of the world, and she has provided them, with prophetic messages of ultimate doom; if people do not receive God in their hearts and change. Mary will be the last attempt by God to remove the cataracts that are causing our blindness in our lives, which is filled with sin and the acceptance of Satan's seductive ways.

Chapter 14

Visions (The Beginning of the Sorrows: 1910-1940)

Both the Old Testament and New Testament describe the condition of society prior to the end of the world. The Old Testament Book of Joel (3:1–2) refers to the last days, when "*the spirit of God will be poured out upon mankind, with sons and daughters prophesying.*" The Apostle Paul also writes in Acts (2:17), "*in the last day that your young men will see visions and old men will dream, dreams*". Paul's reference of old men will "dream, dreams" may be referring to the end time predictions coming from individuals like Nostradamus, Edgar Casey; and even the old Mayan or American Indian cultures. Some of whom were in dream states, as they prophesized. On the other hand, Joel and Paul make reference to sons and daughters prophesying; these may be the boys and girls, who throughout the twentieth century have been seeing visions of the Virgin Mary.

Between the years 1910 and 2010, there have been thousands and perhaps tens of thousands of visions of the Blessed Virgin Mary throughout the world and where 417 individuals have reportedly spoken to her on numerous cases. Not all of the reported visions of Mary have been approved by the Vatican, but others are worthy of belief. In some instances, the Blessed Virgin Mary has been seen daily by numerous people. Most of the apparitions are seen by a single individual, sometimes by several individuals. Currently, the Virgin Mary has been seen by six individuals in Medjugorje for over thirty years. The breakdown of the cases of visionaries per decade is as follows: 1910's (8),

1920s (8) 1930s (49), 1940s (67), 1950s (80), 1960s (43), 1970s (34), 1980s (94), 1990s (32).

The most important apparition of the Virgin Mary was at Fatima, Portugal between the months of May and October of 1917. This was the time when the Blessed Mother of Jesus appeared to Lucia dos Santos, Jacinta and Francisco Marto. She gave them a message for the world, which has since become known as the 'peace plan' from heaven. *"She warned men that if they did not amend their lives, God would be forced to punish them by means of wars and other sufferings."* She revealed to them three secrets pertaining to the world. The Virgin Mary showed them the consequences are Hell for those who do not amend their lives.

1910s

On October 13, 1917, the Virgin Mary provided a miracle to 70,000 pilgrims as proof of her presence there. The day began with rain falling and all the pilgrims went to the Cova da Iria fields at noon, the specified time the Virgin Mary was to appear to Lucia, Francisco and Jacinta. All the pilgrims had become soaked by the rain; according to witnesses the clouds broke and the sun came out and appeared as an opaque spinning disc. The sun appeared to be duller than normal and appeared to cast off multi-colors of light. After a while, the sun looked as if it were plunging towards Earth in a zigzag pattern, frightening all those present. They cried out to the Virgin Mary to save them, and at that moment the sun climbed upward and resumed its place in the sky. All of the pilgrims' wet clothing had suddenly dried during the event. This was a sign from Heaven for us to believe in God, and not to ignore the warnings given by the Virgin Mary.

In the first secret, she accurately predicted World War I was going to end. However, *if men did not stop offending God, another and worse war will begin in the reign of Pius XI...* She told them, when they see a night illumined by an unknown light, it would be a great sign given by God indicating he was about to punish the world by means of war, hunger, and persecution of the Church.

In the second secret, she desired, *"the bishops of the world to consecrate Russia to her immaculate heart, and if not done, Russia would spread her errors throughout the world causing wars and persecutions of the church. The good will be martyred, the Holy Father will have much to suffer and various nations would be annihilated."*

The third secret had two parts. In one part, an angel of God was holding a flaming sword in his hand and was ready to strike the Earth, but the Blessed Mother held him back from doing so, at least for the moment. The other part of the third secret pertained to a future time when the pope, cardinals and bishops were going through a city in half-ruins. They came to a mountain with a huge cross, a place where they are eventually killed by solders.

In the first secret she showed the three children visions of demons and human souls in Hell. This may have been more than a just vision given to the children, it may be an indication that many people are in jeopardy of losing their souls to eternal damnation. It may also be a warning, telling us that the demons from Hell have been released upon the Earth, and they will bring widespread suffering throughout the world.

In Revelation (9:1–6), "*the fifth angel blew his trumpet.... and was given the key to the abyss. He opened the passage and... locust came out of the pit and were given powers to torment mankind, but not to kill them*" Are these locust in reality demons from Hell? Are these demons the cause of wars, genocide, abortions, divorce, greed, hate, immorality, licentiousness, pornography, homosexuality, pedophilia, suicides, homicides, etc.? All of them have been greatly magnified on Earth over the past one hundred years? Was the Virgin Mary warning us these demons were going to over whelm us, if we abandoned God?

The second secret regarding Russia could have not seemed too perilous of a message at the time. Russia consisted of country filled with peasants, being ruled by Emperor Nicholas II. It was an impoverished country without an advance army and barely self-sufficient. However, in October 1917, an evil man named Vladimir Lenin led the revolution that eventually began the spread of communism throughout many places in the world.

Communism would result in tens of millions of people losing their lives through war, genocide and famine. Those who instituted communistic beliefs reaped the most materialistic wealth, at the expense and suffering of the poor. Lenin was a proponent of Karl Marx's philosophies on socialism and religion.

Karl Marx was famously noted for saying, "religion is the opium of the people" and Lenin, who followed that ideology, would spread those errors throughout the world. The USSR denounced any form of religious worship, especially Christianity, and soon church after church would be closed. To worship God in the USSR became illegal, and the government would send tens of thousands of religious leaders to the gulag; to suffer a cruel life of punishment and death.

Although Vladimir Lenin did not live long, seven years after he founded the Soviet Union, an equally evil man named Joseph Stalin eventually took over the country. He maintained and expounded upon the philosophies of Lenin. During Stalin's reign, he initiated the redistribution of food from the Ukraine to Russia. This action resulted in an estimate of five to seven million people in the Ukraine dying of starvation. Stalin, a devout atheist, tried his best to destroy the church single-handedly, but it was none other than Satan behind his attempt. Over a hundred thousand priest, monks and nuns were shot for their religious beliefs. Russia spread its' errors to all of the Soviet Bloc countries, just as the Virgin Mary predicted *"if Russia is not consecrated to my immaculate heart, she will spread her errors throughout the world causing wars and persecution throughout the church."*

The third secret referred to a futuristic time when the world is about to be punished. It also pointed to a time when there would be much distress in the church. In the first part of the secret, the children saw an angel ready to set the world on fire with a sword, but it was held back from doing so. In the second part of the secret, the pope would be walking through a city in half-ruins and he, the bishops and many religious would be killed, by arrows, on top of a mountain that had a huge cross (perhaps at Cross Mountain in Medjugorje).

The first part of that secret is intriguing; an angel of God is about ready to destroy the world with **fire**. God had destroyed the world by a great flood and vowed that he would never destroy the Earth by flood again. However, in the Book of Revelation, there are many mentions of the world being decimated by **fire**, so the declaration of angel holding a flaming sword in this Fatima secret is ominous.

Richard Denis

Visions of fire throughout time and the century

Paul writes in his Second Letter to Peter (3: 3–10), "*in the end times, people will be scoffers and say where is this Jesus that you promise of his coming... The present heavens and Earth have been reserved by the same word for **fire**, kept for the day of judgment of the godless.*" He further writes, "*...the heavens will be dissolved in flames and the elements will be melted by **fire**.*" In the Book of Joel (3:1–2), it was written that God will work wonders in the heavens and Earth and there will be blood, **fires** and columns of smoke with the sun and moon being darkened. Also, it was written in the Book of Zechariah (13:8–9), "*...I will bring one-third through the **fire**...*" In the Book of Revelation (8:7), "*the first angel blew his trumpet and there came hail and **fire** mixed with blood, which was hurled down to Earth. A third of the land was burned up, along with a third of the trees and green grasses*".

During the Fatima vision, the Virgin Mary held back the angel holding the flaming sword, and it may have been an indicator that the world was not going to be destroyed by **fire**, at that time. However, during the twentieth century many visionaries had glimpses of the future where the world was on fire.

A Capuchin priest named Padre Pio was both a stigmatic and visionary, and on February 7, 1950, he had a vision of Jesus who told him, "*Hurricanes of **fire** will pour forth from the clouds and spread over the entire Earth! Storms, bad weather, thunderbolts and earthquakes will cover the Earth for two days. An uninterrupted **rain of fire** will take place! It will begin during a very cold night. All this is to prove that God is the Master of Creation*".

From December 20, 1954 through November 2, 1955 a Ukraine woman named Hanya had seen the Virgin Mary who told her, "*Disaster is upon you as in the times of Noah. Not by flood, but by **fire** the destruction will come. An immense flood of **fire** will destroy the nations for sinning against God. Since the beginning of the world, there has never been such a fall as there is today. This is the kingdom of Satan. I shall dwell on this hill from which I see the entire universe and the many sinners, through this well...*"

More references of destruction by fire have been told by the visionary Sister Mildred Neuzil. On September 24, 1956, the Virgin Mary first appeared to Sister Mildred Mary, as Our Lady of America. She wanted for us to have faith and firmly believe in her love for us, and that she wanted us to be pure of heart. On October 7, 1957, she gave this message to Sister Mildred *"My dear children, either you will do as I desire and reform your lives, or God himself will need to cleanse you in the **fires** of untold punishment. You must be prepared to receive His great gift of peace. If you will not prepare yourselves, God will himself be forced to do so in His justice and mercy."*

On June 1, 1958 in Turzovka, Czechoslovakia, a forester named Matous Lasuta had a vision of our Heavenly Mother. Our Lady signaled Matous to look in the direction of the pines; he looked and saw a tableau showing the globe, then all the different countries on Earth were displayed. Different colors now appeared on the map, some green, some yellow. The water was blue. An inscription explained that the green spots indicate countries where the population is good and the yellow spots denote countries marked for destruction owing to the bad behavior of the people. The high country is greener and the flat land more yellow. Matous saw the yellow invading and covering more countries while the green is retreating. The message was that the world is getting worse and worse… Then powerful explosions burst forth over the water and land. A dense rain of small leaves fall to the Earth, and upon reaching the ground, these turned into ***flames***. Soon all the touched soil is covered by ***fire***. Matous saw this as "a punishment by God".

During the period from June 1, 1961 through November 15, 1965, four young girls (Conchita, Jacinta, Mari Loli and Mari Cruz) from Garabandal, Spain saw the Virgin Mary. She told them that the world would soon experience global chastisements. These events would be in four stages and the Blessed Virgin Mary referred to them as "the end of times." The visionary Mari Loli described this dreadful event, "We were absolutely terrified… I cannot find words to explain it… We saw the rivers turn to blood… **Fire** was falling from heaven… And something worse still, which

I cannot reveal at this time." According to the visionaries, God will give mankind several chances to change before he sends the chastisement, but before the punishment there will be **warning** given to mankind followed by a miracle. The visionary Conchita knows the date of this "miracle" and will announce its coming eight days in advance. As of 2011, she is fifty-five years old.

In 1984, Betania, Venezuela, Maria Esperanza, who bears the stigmata was told by the Virgin Mary *"today in these times, He with me, wishes to renew consciences because mankind is currently abusing graces received and is moving towards perdition, and if there is no change and improvement in life, he will succumb under **fire**, war and death…"*

An Italian seer named Elena Leonardi was shown, on April 1, 1976, a vision by the Virgin Mary of an unforeseen **fire** that had descended upon the whole Earth and a great part of humanity was destroyed.

In the same timeframe, a Yugoslavian visionary named Julka was also shown a vision of the world on fire. She saw it as various stages of a chastisement, the first begin with a warm wind followed by ten claps of thunder, which appeared to shake the whole world. She then saw the air on **fire** as if it were a **gigantic sheet of flame**. After that event, the sun turned "red as blood", then darkness followed.

In 1981, three youths (17-year-old Alphonsine, 20-year-old Nathalie, and 21-year-old Marie Claire) from Kibeho, Rwanda were given glimpses of the future by the Blessed Virgin Mary. The visionaries were shown **trees in flame**, a river of blood and corpses piled on top of each other.

In 1982, an interior locution (message) was given to Father Stefano Gobi, a priest from Milan, Italy, by the Virgin Mary. Mary was quoted as saying, *"The hour of justice and mercy has begun and soon you will see the wonders of the merciful love of the Divine Heart of Jesus and the triumph of my immaculate heart."* Furthermore she said, *"Humanity has reached that time when it is to live through the bloody hours of the great scourge which will purify it through **fire**, hunger and devastation."*

All of these visions of a world on **fire** could mean that the world is getting progressively closer to the event, when the angel of God will sweep the Earth with his sword of fire. The visionaries described the sky on fire as if it were a sheet of flames. Could this possibly be the result of the sun ejecting a mass of plasma? Scientists have claimed that the sun is going through a cycle with the sun spots maximizing in the year 2013; if so, it could be the time of the great judgment by God.

It appears the Virgin Mary was attempting to withhold God's judgment and save as many souls as possible. Perhaps, we are in a time of grace, and the period in time where the sheep are being separated from the goats. This would corroborate with Jesus's parables where, at harvest time the wheat and tares are being separated. Once the tares are separated, they are thrown into the **fire** to be burnt.

The second part of this third Fatima secret mentioned is a city, in half-ruins. Is this a city actually destroyed or is it symbolic of the Catholic Church being half-destroyed; due to its parishioners no longer following their Catholic faith? What would lead more than 50% of the Catholics to lose their faith? In the mid-1980s, there were cases being reported of priest molesting children. The number of cases exploded into the thousands of abuses by priest throughout the world. Cases were reported in the heart of the Catholic Church in places like Ireland, America, France, Belgium and Germany. These sex abuse scandals resulted in many people losing and abandoning, not only their faith in the Catholic Church, but in God.

Was perhaps the vision of the pope walking in a city in half-ruins symbolic to the Catholic Church being decimated by the actions of these priests? Will Rome be attacked and destroyed, perhaps by terrorists? Lucia had said that the third message would be a better understood if it was revealed in the 1960s, which coincides with the timeframe of these child molestations. One must ask this question, were child molestations always present in the church, or did they transpire only around the 1950s? Satan found a crack in the armor of God's priests. Satan preyed upon these men, who try with much difficulty to remain abstinent; so if these godly men, who are close to God, become subjected to Satan's temptations, where does this leave mankind? Are we any better than them?

The visions and messages reported at Fatima, accurately predicted WWI ending, a sky of illuminated by an unknown light preceded WWII, and the current persecution of the church. There have been many other visions in the twentieth century; some were of Jesus, while most were of Mary. Some visions had no messages (or they were never revealed), some visions were of the Virgin Mary bringing comfort to the inhabitants of Earth; still other visions were dire warnings of punishments. All of these visions were for a purpose, mainly to inform the world that God really does exists.

1920s

In the 1920s there were eight reported visionaries claiming to see and talk to the Blessed Virgin Mary. These visions took place in Canada, France, Spain and Brazil. It was a period of rebuilding from World War I, and when mankind began to focus on their new god 'money'; they placed God aside for materialistic things, purchased with money. Money could buy all happiness, so they thought.

One of the visions, reported by Sister Elisabetta Redaelli in 1924, was that of the Virgin Mary holding the infant Jesus in her arms. Sister Elisabetta was perfectly healthy until at the age of twenty-five when she started suffering from meningitis; followed by pulmonary tuberculosis, progressive muscular paralysis. She stated I saw His cheeks; He trembled as if He were grief-stricken, and was weeping. When Elisabetta asked why He was weeping the Virgin Mary replied, *"The infant Jesus is weeping because He is not sufficiently loved, sought out and desired, even by people who are consecrated to Him ..."* At the end of the visions Elisabetta was cured of all of her illnesses.

Perhaps this vision of the Virgin Mary was actually a **warning,** and that Elisabetta's symptoms represent mankind who becomes infatuated with the things of this world. That in time, we allow materialistic things to become more important than God. Just as an infection enters the body trying to destroy it, evil becomes like an infection. Evil begins to paralyze us, not from moving, but rather where we no longer want to receive the word of God. Just as Elisabetta became physically blinded, we become eventually blinded by the desires for wealth and eventually we no longer see the truth. The Blessed Virgin Mary may have been warning us the lust of money glittering in our eyes and hearts, as seen in the 1920s, will lead us away from the Jesus. Maybe like Elisabetta was cured, Mary was saying that the cure for this illness of lust for materialistic things can be overcome by loving Jesus and God.

1930s

The number of reported visions of the Virgin Mary jumped from eight in the 1920s to forty-nine in the 1930s. All of these visions of Mary, with the exception of one, were in Belgium, Spain, Germany and France. The 1930s were an ominous time; the world was entrenched in depression, countries were in political flux, communism was taking over, and one Fascist country was building up a mighty war machine. It was time for the Virgin Mary to come on the scene, more than ever, to warn us of the evil entering our world, and what was soon going to befall us.

Satan was on the prowl, and working in the hearts of many men. He was corrupting our minds, and was out to destroy the peoples of all nations. The world needed healing and guidance, a way out of the quagmire that it was headed into. On June 30, 1931, in a little known province known as Guipúzcoa, located in the autonomous Basque Country of northern Spain, a brother and sister from Ezkioga – Antonia, age 11, and Andrés, age 7, saw the Blessed Virgin Mary. She warned them that Spain would soon be in a civil war with much blood being spilled and for them to pray and pray. Although this vision was not approved by the church at that time, Spain did have a civil war that began in the year 1936, and did not end until 1939. This was just the beginning of many wars in the twentieth century.

There were numerous visions of the Virgin Mary throughout Belgium during that timeframe. In late September of 1933, in a village called Onkerzele, Belgium, Leonie van den Dyck saw the Virgin Mary, who was very sad. She told her *"Pray, pray a lot… her country was in grave danger."* Again on February 3, 1934, the virgin Mary appeared to her and said, *"I'll will repeat what I want: I want that here, you establish stations of the cross in honor of my sorrows …*

Richard Denis

All those depicting the Sacred Head of my Son carry, will be protected..."
Protected from what?

On January 1, 1933, Adolf Hitler entered the coalition government as chancellor and a few years later he became dictator of Germany. Seven years later on May 10, 1940, the Nazi's marched through Belgium without much resistance. German soldiers were in Belgium and many Jews, being under the control of the Nazis, were deported to the concentration camps. However, as the war wore on and during the months of December 16, 1944 to January 28, 1945, a ferocious battle was taking place in the Ardennes Forest (near Bastogne) located in Belgium. It was known as the "Battle of the Bulge", and at the end of this battle, over 112,000 allied and German forces died along with having much causality on both sides. The tears of the Virgin Mary must have been flowing for the many young men had died.

The Virgin Mary was also seen at Banneux, Belgium. On February 11, 1933, Mariet Beco received a message from the Virgin Mary, who told her *"I have come to relieve suffering."* Once more the Virgin Mary appears to indicating there would be much suffering in Belgium. Although there was no warning of an upcoming war given to the visionary, the Virgin Mary provided a miraculous spring. It would heal illnesses not only the people of Belgium, but also for people in the world. Perhaps, this miraculous spring was not only meant to heal physical ailments, but possibly it symbolized a spiritual healing "a way out of our ungodly ways". Healing, the world would need in the future; requiring humanity to come back to God, and to be healed from the evil that had taken over our lives.

Also in 1933, the Virgin Mary appeared to five young children: Andree and Gilberte Degeimbre (ages 15 and 9), Fernande, Golberte and Albert Voisin (ages 15, 13 and 11) at Beauraing, Belgium. Her message was *"I shall convert sinners."* It was a simple message, one of hope for all sinners that had have strayed from God in this century. This same message of conversion will be renewed with the Medjugorje messages given in the 2000s.

Between November 1, 1937 and November 3, 1940, Mary appeared over a hundred times at Heede, Germany to four girls, ages 12 to 14-years-old. The girls, Anna Schulte, Greta Gansferth, Margaret Gansferth, and Susanna Bruns were given foreboding messages of the future. She told them, *"It is my will that my message is released literally. A small group will get the message correctly and carried out. Most people will ignore it, but will reject and resent it. But fear not, I'm with you. These times require atonement. If you pray I'll see the rest."* Mary was appearing in the heart of Germany, a country lead by evil men, who would soon commit atrocities throughout the face of the world. She was pleading for the atonement for the sins of the world, and they were being ignored.

A number of years later, Jesus appeared to these visionaries, and gave them this message, *"Humanity has not listened to my Blessed Mother, who appeared in Fatima to call for penance. Now I come, I myself at this late hour to warn the world. I'm very close ... The Earth will tremble terribly. A trial in small! But you do not fear. I am with you. Be glad and I thank you. Those who expect to have my help, my grace and my love. But for those who are not in a state of grace will be awful. The angels of justice are now scattered around the four cardinal points. I will make known to mankind. All souls recognize me as their God. It is five minutes before twelve. I come, I'm at the door! Humanity will regret."*

Jesus's reference to the time being five minutes before twelve infers the beginning of a new era, is close at hand. The new era is being represented as twelve o'clock, the beginning of a new day. Jesus also said, *"What will happen is terrible, as never seen since the world began. I come manifested as myself and my will ... My daughters; I am coming soon, very soon. The Blessed Virgin Mary and the choirs of angels intervene in all these events. Hell is confident of victory, but I know I will take it from their hands. I will allow rain of misfortunes on the world, because in this way it will save many. Blessed are those who suffer from all of those who offend me. I come and peace will come with me. With a small number of elected I will build my kingdom. It will come like lightning, suddenly, sooner than you think ..."*

Another message by Jesus was *"Men refuse my mercy, my love and my merits. Humanity is worse than before the flood, dying in the quagmire of sin. Hatred and greed guide their hearts, all though Satan. This generation deserves to be annihilated but only just looking at my mercy, I will succeed."* Jesus moreover said, *"Humanity will recognize my power and I will show them my righteousness and my mercy. My dear children, the hour is coming more and more. Pray tirelessly and do not be confused. I gather my elect who converge simultaneously from all sides the world and glorify me. I come. Happy are those who are ready, happy that I hear."*

All the messages given to visionaries regarding the end times will finalize within our lifetimes. These messages given by Jesus Himself are the direst of warnings, in that humanity needs to turn back to God, or else suffer the consequences. Note that Jesus said that he is gathering His elect from the whole world. Only at the end times is the wheat (elect) gathered together. Jesus continually refers to time being short and His reference of five minutes before the hour of twelve may represent 99.9% of mankind's allotted time has passed.

Our opportunity to convert is down to a trickle amount of time and Jesus's coming can be at any moment; today, tomorrow, or next year. Once He comes; those who have been sitting on the fence, as the old saying goes, will no longer be allowed to decide at that point in time to side with Jesus. There will always be skeptics who'll wait and see; those in the past that lived and died without seeing His return must have felt that they got away with it, but not really. Their souls will be judged the same way as nonbelievers.

It has been said that all the culminations necessary for the end times will occur in the lifetime of one person, but what defines the length of a lifetime? If we are calculating that the beginning of the last days was initiated in May, 1917 then we are projecting the end to be around the year 2017. That would mean an individual would be one hundred years old, and certainly there are individuals who have lived that long. However, if the beginning of those days coincided with the re-establishment of Israel in 1947, then an individual would only be seventy years old in 2017. In either case, it is conceivable that all of these events can happen in the lifetime of a person.

As mentioned, God will not yell "time is up"; instead as the final event becomes closer to becoming a reality, the number of messages from Heaven will become more frequent and alarming. And from the 1940s to our current day, messages have been pouring out of Heaven like a deluge.

There have been miracles healings for the faithful, there are visionaries who speak to the Virgin Mary and in some cases on a daily basis for decades; there are religious statues, paintings, and religious cards of Jesus and Mary weeping tears and also blood.

These events are taking place worldwide with little or no attention given to them by our media.

There has been a case where millions of people saw the Virgin Mary every night for over a year in Zeitoun, Egypt, and it was never reported on American television. Even evangelist like Billy Graham is warning his congregation of Jesus's coming. All of this can be reviewed on the internet, so for those skeptics who say they never heard that God is attempting to convert us, are closing their eyes, ears, and heart to the Holy Spirit. Proclamation of ignorance will not help them.

Chapter 15

Visions (The Pot of Water is on the Stove: 1940s)

By the 1940s, Europe was already at war and within another year, the rest of the world would be in the fray. The war caused many changes in society, and the Virgin Mary was trying hard us guide away from our new fond evil life styles. She appeared to sixty-three visionaries in the 1940s, most of them being in Europe, with some in Asia, South America and even the USA. Her messages during this time consisted of warnings of impending chastisements, if people don't return back to God.

1940s

Some of Mary's most serious messages were given to a woman named Ida Peerdman, who lived in Amsterdam, Holland. In 1945, Ida Peerdman, and her three sisters were at home when a priest, who was a friend of the family stopped by for a visit. While they were conversing, Ida, the youngest of the four sisters, noticed something in the adjacent room. She got up and saw an immense light appearing, and her surroundings seemed to fade away. From the light she saw a female figure, dressed in white, who began to speak to her. It was the Virgin Mary.

Throughout the 1940-50s, Ida Peerdman had visions of the Blessed Virgin Mary, who showed her futuristic events and gave her fifty-six messages. The messages were grave and often the Virgin Mary would be seen crying, crying for the sorrowful condition of humanity. There were selected messages about countries like the

United States, England, Russia, China and Korea. Some of these messages alluded to a future war between these nations, others referred to natural disasters, while still others were indicators of a falling away (apostasy) from God.

The Virgin Mary's message on Feb 25, 1946, pointed to disasters and as Ida indicated she looks terribly sad. Her message was, *"disaster upon disaster, natural disasters."* Then I saw the words *'Hunger' and 'Political Chaos'*. The Virgin Mary said, *"This goes not only for your country, but for the whole world."* In June of that same year in the presence of Our Lady, Ida saw the globe and the Virgin Mary pointed at it. Ida saw glaring lights and rays, **and the globe seemed to explode on all sides.** Then the Virgin Mary pointed at the sky. She stood to Ida's right side, and she pointed to the east. Ida saw a great number of stars in the sky, and the Virgin Mary said, *"That is where it comes from."* This message is reminiscent to the star from the Book of Revelation (8:10), which falls from the sky after the third angel blew his trumpet. Is this 'star' close enough to Earth that it will fall upon us in the near future?

On December 7, 1947, Ida was given a vision of heavy, thick clouds appearing over Europe and under them huge waves engulfing the continent. She wrote, "I saw the Virgin Mary standing in a glaring, bright light. Her face had become drawn and she looks very sad. She pointed at those heavy clouds and waves, and said, *"They will first have to perish by that flood, and only then …"* and I saw those words written down. After the words "only then" I saw many dots, as if something was to follow, but must remain hidden. The Virgin Mary's face brightens, and I saw the water evaporate as steam. For a moment the sun seems to break through. Again the Virgin Mary pointed out the Earth to me, and I noticed that everything had cleared up. And I saw lots of bones of human beings scattered over the ground, parts of skulls, arms and legs. It was a horrible sight. I heard the Virgin Mary say, *"This is the perdition. But go and work, work …"*

Was this vision denoting that Europe is going to experience a great flood, perhaps caused by this "exploding globe"? Large fragments from this globe could hit the oceans and cause massive tsunamis throughout Europe. Was the cloud from nuclear devices, or is it a metaphorical one? Perhaps the cloud represents people that have strayed away from God and can no longer see the truth.

The flood may represent evil being poured upon the Earth, causing human beings to lose their souls by obeying Satan.

December 26, 1947, Ida had another vision, one which she did not understand and contained a very peculiar scene. She wrote, "I looked at the sky, and something seems to be launched into it. There is something flying past me so rapidly that I can hardly see it. It is shaped like a cigar or a torpedo, and its color is like that of aluminum. All of a sudden I saw something shooting off from the back of it. At first I feel total numbness, I live, and yet I do not live. Then I saw horrible images of people before me. I saw faces, white faces, covered with dreadful ulcers, something like leprosy. Then I feel terrible deadly diseases something like cholera, leprosy—everything those people will have to suffer". Suddenly that is gone again, and I saw tiny little black things floating about me. I tried to feel what it is, but it was not possible. It seems to be very fine matter. With my eyes I cannot discern what it was. It is as if I would have to look through something, and below I now saw brilliant white fields. Upon those fields I see those little black things, but enlarged, and it was as if they were alive. I don't know how to describe this properly. I ask the Virgin Mary, "Are these bacilli?" She answers very seriously, *"It is hellish."* Then I felt my face and my whole body swelling. It felt like my face got very bloated, and everything was stiff and swollen. I could not move. I heard the Virgin Mary say, *"And that is what they are inventing,"* and then very softly, *"not only Russian, but the others as well."* After this the Virgin Mary said emphatically, *"Peoples, be warned!"*

Ida, without comprehending what it is she saw, is apparently depicting the launching of a nuclear missile. What makes this unusual is that rockets had only been briefly used by the Nazis just a few years prior to Ida's vision. She also appears to be describing a futuristic war, in a time when people are suffering from either radiation sickness or from biological weapons. Could this event be the outbreak of World War III? Are the Russians or Chinese going to war against America? Are terrorists or a renegade country, like Iran or Korea going to use nuclear or biological weapons, as a means to promote their idealistic philosophies? Is this why the Blessed mother told Ida "be warned", warned about the Koreans, Russian, radical Islamists, and Asians?

Another grim message about the possible use of biological weapons by the Russians was given to Ida on October 1, 1949. The Virgin Mary said, *"Come along to Russia."* I saw Russia and she took me along to glass buildings, underground too—all kinds of people are working there. There seems to be Germans, Frenchmen, Poles, and others too. I heard many of them speaking different languages. These buildings seemed to be deep in Russia, somewhere in the great, uninhabited plains of northern Russia. The Virgin Mary said, **"They are making chemicals there. America, be warned!** *Intervene, do intervene!"* Not only human lives are at issue here, but higher powers. *"Bring faith into the world again. But the faithful ..."* and the Virgin Mary shook her head.

On May 7, 1949, Ida had a vision, in which she saw Europe lying before her and next to it, America. It was as if she could seize something from the middle of North America and sprinkle it over Europe. I did not know what it was. Then in the distance I saw a multitude of Eastern peoples. ***"These he will rouse"***, said the Virgin Mary. I saw this in the far distance. Then a skull appeared, and I heard the Virgin Mary say, **"A great disaster will occur."** The use of the words 'sprinkling over Europe and Eastern people' could be referring to Middle Eastern peoples. The phrase "these he will rouse" could indicate that Satan will rouse the Muslim peoples and perhaps have them start a holy war against the West.

Shortly after World War II on May 25, 1946, in Marienfried, Germany another woman was receiving messages from the Blessed Virgin Mary. Her name was Bärbel Ruess, who was twenty-two years old when she received three messages from the Virgin Mother. In one of the Virgin Mother's message, she was told, *"... This is why the Father poured his cup of wrath on the peoples because they rejected his Son (rejection of the Christ by the Antichrist and his allies). The world has been dedicated to my immaculate heart, but the consecration became for many a terrifying responsibility (because of the abandon of faith and testimony even by the Christian religious and political leaders) ... so that the* **Christ can reign soon as the King of Peace***. The world must drink the chalice of wrath until the dregs because of the innumerable sins that offended His heart.* **The star of the abysses will rise more furious than ever and will make terrifying because it knows its time is short...**" Mary said again, *"that the devil will have in the world such a big power, that all those who would not be firmly established in her would* let themselves be lead astray, because he will know how to blind men, that even the best would let themselves be seduced (the chiefs of churches, in head, the pope who is misled by the star)."

This vision was a preface of what was to come upon the Earth; Satan has been given immense power and he has little time to misguide humanity. Even men of power, knowledge and wisdom cannot stop the power of Satan. Only those who have dedicated themselves to Jesus and Mary will not be misled by Satan. This was a warning of chastisements that God was soon going to allow Satan to tempt humanity and only the most devout will survive.

Another vision on June 25, 1946, Mary told Bärbel Ruess, *"I am the Great Mediator of graces…I want to make miracles secretly, in the souls, until the number of sacrifices is complete. It is given to you to shorten the days of darkness. Your prayers and yours sacrifices **will annihilate the image of the Beast**… Offer me lots of sacrifices! Make of your prayers a sacrifice! Be selfless! …The opinions will divide about this message, **a great number will be shocked**, but a small legion will understand it well and will spread it. They will recognize my will and will rejoice. This legion has recognized my position in this time and has given me great joy. This legion has its representatives in many countries… Many among them have already seen my secret miracles."*

The Virgin Mary is using apocalyptic words like "sacrifices will annihilate the image of the beast." The beast is annihilated only during the end times and Mary further says those individuals not believing in her messages will be "shocked". Shocked could infer human beings will be in denial when they see their world destroyed. They will not comprehend that all their accumulated gold, silver, and money will not have any value. They will realize their lives were wasted chasing the worthless things of this world, and they failed to store up treasure in Heaven. Jesus said in Matthew (6:19-21), *"do not store up for yourselves treasures on Earth, where moth and decay destroy, and thieves break in and steal. But store up treasures in heaven, where neither moth nor decay destroys, nor thieves break in and steal. For where your treasure is, so will your hearts be"*.

She was also referring to small legions recognizing her position. Can this be reference to those individuals who have listened to the visionaries (especially the Medjugorje visionaries) and have converted? This legion that prays to God will also pray the Rosary is known to be present in every country of the world.

In the spring of 1947, while praying in the chapel of the local hospital in Montichiari, Nurse Pierina Gilli had an unforgettable experience. Mary, the Mother of God, appeared to her in a wonderful vision, as the exalted Lady, who was very sad and had tears in her eyes. Pierina noticed that Mary's heart was pierced by three swords. The first sword stood for the unworthy celebration of Holy Mass and communion, the second sword stood for the priest being unfaithful and giving up their vocation, the third sword stood for betrayal of the faith. Pierina said, "Our Lady asked for prayer, sacrifice, and penance."

Those were her only words. It appears these swords were a prediction of a future time, when people would go to church, and go through all the rites, but remain unrepentant of their evil ways. They represent a time when there is such a great loss in faith; that not only will people disregard the church, but young men would disregard priestly vocations, it may represent the time when the priests (betrayers of faith) molested children.

On her third apparition on October 22, 1947, Pierina saw Our Lady again in the chapel of the hospital in the presence of many staff members, doctors, and people from the town. This time, Our Lady requested her desired devotion to be realized. She said, *"I have placed myself as the mediatrix between my Divine son and mankind, especially for the soul consecrated to God. Tired of the continuous offenses,* **He already wanted to dispense his justice.***"*

The Fourth Apparition on November 16, 1947, Our Lady appeared at the Basilica of Montichiari, in the presence of some people, among them were several priests. Pierina heard the words *"Our Lord can no longer watch the many grievous sins against purity.* **He wants to send a flood of punishments***. I have interceded that He may be merciful once more! Therefore, I ask for prayer and penance to atone for these sins."* Pierina replied to Our Lady's request with a devoted "Yes". The Blessed Virgin added, *"I lovingly ask the priest to express their great love and stop the people from committing those sins. Whoever will atone for those sins will receive my blessings and graces."* In reply, the seer questioned whether we may hope for forgiveness, Our Lady said, *"Yes, as long as these sins are no longer committed."* With these words she went away.

In 1947, the Blessed Virgin Mary prevented the world from being punished by God though her intercessions, and to stave off future punishments; we have to pray and do penance. The world had already gone through a war, and there was massive destruction. One could only imagine what punishments God has in store for the ungrateful, those who benefited from Mary's intercessions, but did not change. Mary's intercessions will soon come to an end, and the fury of God will be unstoppable. If God had graciously given mankind additional time to change because of Mary, and we didn't heed her, an unfathomable number of disasters await us in the near future.

On November 12, 1949, a 40-year old woman from Wisconsin named Mary Van Hoof reported receiving a vision from the Blessed Virgin Mary. In subsequent visions she was told to bring the truth to people through prayer and the rosary. The messages also made references to an imminent chastisement, a thermonuclear World War III, Soviet submarines, and accusations that the mainstream Roman Catholic hierarchy and papacy had been subverted.

Throughout the 1940s, the Virgin Mary had given us warnings about chastisements and future wars. Was not the destruction from World War II enough to redirect us away from future devastation? Through prayer and penance; chastisements can be averted. However, our arrogance and desire for "the good life" has clouded mankind's faith in a living God. All these warnings will most likely be swept aside by humanity and therefore we can expect only the worse for our future.

Chapter 16

Visions (The Water is Warming: 1950-70s)

The 1950s were a prosperous time for Americans and life was filled with pleasures. Europe was rebuilding and a new attitude was developing as well. At this time of peace and prosperity, the Virgin Mary was reportedly seen by eighty visionaries. Of those eighty reported visionaries, forty of them were in Italy. Perhaps the Virgin Mary was warning the Catholic Church of the chastisements soon to come upon them, in the form of pedophile priests.

1950s

The visions of Ida Peerdman continued into the 1950s and her vision on August 15, 1950 was focused towards the orient. Ida described the vision as, "Suddenly I saw a beast before me—a symbolic beast—which is unfamiliar to me. After that I saw crabs and big starfish. Next, I saw an island before me, and I am given to understand that it is Formosa. A smaller island lies further down. I heard something come from the left and make a swooping action over the island. I heard the words, *"America, take warning here!"* I felt that something is to happen on that island."

Formosa, also known as Taiwan, is the place where General Chiang Kai-shek and his Nationalist forces fled to in 1949, after being beaten by Mao Tse-tung and his communistic party during the Chinese Civil War. China has always made claim to Taiwan, but America's presence in the region has prevented them from acquiring the land by military action. It appears that Ida's description of the beast is Communistic Red China, and the warning to America may be that China will try to forcible take Taiwan. Recently, China has warned the United States not to interfere with Taiwan. Can this be what the Virgin Mary was alluding too?

In April 15, 1951, Ida had been given a vision of the world being overrun by creatures. She writes, "And now the Lady lets me see the world and it is as if snakes were creeping all over the globe. Then she said, *"People still do not realize what a serious plight the world is in. Because people are becoming so shallow, they cannot realize how much harm this is doing to their faith."* After this the Lady looked in front of herself for a long time, as if gazing far into the distance. Then she said, *"Child, these times are the same as the times before the Son came. That is why I cannot insist enough that people, that Rome, that everyone help fight for the cause of the Son. I know that there is some revival here and there, but far from what is needed to save the world. And* **the world must be saved from degeneration, disaster and war**. *Send this prayer and image to those countries where faith has declined."*

By her knowing the future of mankind, the Virgin Mary was attempting to warn us to stay away from the things in this world that distract us from our faith. The world had become like ancient Rome, filled with money, lust, excessiveness, gluttony, selfishness, materialism, pleasure, and leisure. Every culture, every country, every race and every belief has been affected with these things. We had become so shallow by placing these things as priorities over God. In doing this, we would further lose our faith in God, and the result would be imminent disaster.

August 15, 1951, the Virgin Mary told Ida, *"I have said: disasters will come, natural disasters. I have said: the great ones will disagree with one another. I have said:* **the world is falling into degeneration**. *That is why the Father and the Son now sends the Lady back into the world as she was."* The Lady known as just Mary further said, *"The world is falling into degeneration, it is in degeneration."* and on March 28, 1952, she said, *"Do you know, child, what kind of an era this is?* **Throughout the centuries the world has not yet experienced such an era, such a decline of faith**; *and that is why I want this to be carried out, quickly and without fear. Tell your spiritual director that in these modern times, in this modern world, which knows so well how to act promptly and quickly in material affairs, it is equally necessary in spiritual matters to act quickly, promptly and in a modern way."*

Mary continues to warn us that if humanity proceeds on the path of degeneration; eventually we will have to pay the price by the means of disasters. She has been warning humanity for sixty years; instead of changing our ways, we have been merrily following a path leading to ruin. Note, that she was concerned with the loss of faith. In the 1950s, 74% of all Americans went to church, now it is <40%; regardless of denomination. Some pollsters report only 20% of people regularly went to church in 2011.

Mary's message to Ida on March 20, 1953, *"In order to prove that I am the Lady of All Nations, I will tell you:* **great powers will fall; politico-economic struggle will arise;** *watch out for the false prophets;* **pay attention to the meteors***; there will be disasters; there will be natural disasters; we are facing great decisions; we are facing heavy pressure."*

In 1953, there were two super powers being the United States and USSR. In the 1990s, the USSR disbanded and Mary's reference to a time when there will be politico-economic struggles has been on the world's center stage throughout the last decade. Countries are falling in the Middle East and there also have been many commonplace struggles within the European community. These struggles are real, and there are individuals who are attempting to use the name of God as a means for them to take control of the free world. Many people are being deceived by these false prophets, who have been taking control of Middle East countries and their plans are to destabilize the world.

In addition, Mary referred to natural disasters and to be watchful for meteors. Her message indicates these events will take place at the same time. Certainly, in the year 2011, there have been numerous natural disasters and political upheaval. The only thing that has not been fulfilled is for the meteor to strike Earth, but one may be on its way to strike us soon.

One of Ida's last messages was on May 31, 1955, the Virgin Mother said, *"Satan is not yet expelled. The* **Lady of All Nations may now come in order to expel Satan***. She comes to announce the Holy Spirit. The* **Holy Spirit will then come over this Earth***. You, however, shall pray my prayer which I gave to the world. Every day and every moment you shall think of the prayer which the Lady of All Nations gave to this world in this time. How strongly Satan is ruling, God alone knows. He now sends his Mother, the Lady of All Nations, to you, to all nations.*

She will defeat Satan, as has been foretold. She will place her feet upon Satan's head."

The mention that Mary has "*come in order to expel Satan and will place her feet upon Satan's head*" are once more a warning that we are living in the final days of Earth. Mary's foot upon Satan's head is symbolic of his defeat. His defeat is after the days of tribulation, a time when most of the Earth and humanity have been destroyed. However, her message gives one of hope in that the Holy Spirit will be coming upon the Earth to regenerate a new spirit for those who are receptive to Him. This new found desire to love God can equate to the time when God is collecting His elect from the four corners of the world at the end times. Once they are collected, the remainders of the souls are to be sent to the fires of Hell.

In 1953, the Blessed Virgin appeared to three children; Juan Angel Collado and his sisters Ramonita e Isidra Belén were seven, eight and nine-years-old. They lived in Sabana Grande Rincon, Puerto Rico. She told them, *"The **hour will come** when the spiritual and **moral deterioration of the shepherds of my Son's flock will be** a matter of **public knowledge**. The indifference of God's children will prevent them from seeing the great danger which lies in wait. The pain in my heart will be all the more piercing, since it will be the sign that the time has come for making known the following message "difficult and confused those times will be. **Spiritual growth will become very, very difficult for the sons and daughters of God**. There will come further times when such growth will seem almost impossible. **Strange ideas and new philosophies will enshroud the true way in greater darkness**. The teachings of my most Beloved Son, the order established by the Father and truth itself, will be set aside in favour of these new and strange beliefs. The selfishness of God's children will give rise to conflicts and divisions which will intensify my pain. You must realize that the shepherds of the flock are men as well. Pardon their faults and assist them, for they represent my Son. Remain steadfast in the true way to the Father; in the Church of my Son; for times of great testing are drawing near."*

The Blessed Mother message "*spiritual and moral deterioration of the shepherds of my Son's flock*" is a straightforward reference to the priest, who sexually molested young children and was made public in the late 1990s. This message, however, was given in 1953, when nobody could understand what she was talking about. So if this was revealed in 1953, her other message about a spiritual darkness and confusion coming into the world must also be true. During this time, more people will continually fall away from the faith; the things of this world are drawing more souls away from God, so we must be prepared for this time of *great testing*.

In another message to the children she said, *"Humanity has submerged itself in a very deep and profound indifference; it lacks faith, hope and love.* **The ego, selfishness, materialism and blasphemous murmurs have corrupted the hearts of many**. *The demon has penetrated the very souls of many men on their true way. A very great danger is threatening humanity. My new children remain alert."*

During another message in 1953, Our Lady said, *"Those will be difficult times of great* **social and moral deterioration**, *but above all of* **spiritual deterioration. Men's selfishness will reign**. *In the moments of greater tribulation and persecution I will send the angel that will show you the way, again. This is the sign that the time has come to make the following message known:* **Thousands of souls are lost daily**, **dragged by sin** *and infidelity away from my most Beloved Son. The social, moral and spiritual deterioration darkens humanity that populates the Earth. The* **prophesied times** *in which* **parents and children destroy themselves have arrived. Humanity is plunged in a great crisis of faith hardly noticed**. *Most men do not keep their Christian commitments. Driven by selfishness and pride they have fallen in the deceit of appearances and superficiality of human demands. Some priests, ministers of my Son as shepherds of the flock are irreverent in the celebration of the Holy Sacraments; they become allies of the enemy by the infidelity to their consecrated life, their attachment to money, the search for recognition and their unrestraint to pleasures. They are responsible for the* **loss of the faith**; *they motivate falling away and engender antagonism and violence. If they do not repent and start a life of penance, they will lose their souls forever.* **It is the hour, in which you have, because you have not responded to my warnings, the prophecies will start to come true**. *My children protect yourselves under my mantle and live in my virtues. I warn you that one day the vault of heaven will be totally orange and dark, there will be an intense cold and* **a great tribulation and desperation will fall over mankind. It will be as if Hell had settled upon Earth. Parents, children and all human beings will fight among themselves and will want to kill each other**. *They will hunt each other until death. …Many will the alleged apparitions be. Some will be genuine and others will be the* *work of the evil one that with sagacity and disguise of light, will involve many..."*

If the alarms are not sounding off by now, what will it take for the Virgin Mary to bring us back to God? In 1953, she was talking about the deterioration of our society, as seen by the selfishness of mankind who idolizes and worships money. She speaks of the loss of faith, a time when people will no longer go to church and believe in God. Her messages are if she is reading the headlines in our current daily newspapers that reports news of murder, rebelliousness, greed, etc. from all over the world. She is once more warning us that we are approaching apocalyptic times and indeed we are seeing many things being revealed in our time. Satan remains out there mocking God, by teaching people to indulge in sin. He may even appear as the Virgin Mary, to discourage people from believing in authentic apparitions. Humanity is still trying to find the end of the rainbow, and Satan has seduced us to believe we live in a perfect world, when it is anything but paradise.

Sister Elena Aiello of Consenza, Italy received messages from Our Lord Jesus Christ and the Blessed Mother from 1959 until 1961. On Good Friday in 1950, she received this message, **"Satan reigns and triumphs on Earth! See how the souls are falling into hell.** *See how high the flames are, and the* **souls, who fall into them like flakes of snow, look like transparent embers**! *How many sparks! How many cries of hate, and of despair! How much pain! See how* **Russia will burn**! *Before my eyes there extended an immense field covered with flames and smoke, in which souls were submerged as if in a sea of fire! And all this fire,"* concluded the Madonna. In addition she said, *"Is not that which will fall from the hands of men, but will be hurled directly from the Angels* **(at the time of the great chastisement or 'housecleaning' that will come upon the Earth)**. *Therefore, I ask prayers, penance and sacrifice, so I may act as Mediatrix for My Son in order to save souls."*

Our Mother in Heaven is warning us that our souls are in peril; they are falling into hell as if they were snowflakes, not being pure white, but as transparent burning embers. Many souls are falling into the abyss, and a great chastisement of fire will be hurled down to Earth by the angels in the near future. How many times has she warned humanity of this coming? How many visionaries throughout the world have quoted her words of punishment by fire, and that the fire will not be set by man, but will come from by the hands of the angels. The angels are the ones who have been given control over the objects in the universe and now they are waiting to send that ball of fire upon the Earth at God's command. Yet nobody is listening to the words that will save us from these disasters. The words are to convert and pray.

Sister Mildred Mary Neuzil was born in Brooklyn, New York and received messages from the Virgin Mary, who called herself Our Lady of America. Our Lady's message to her in January 1957, *"The hour grows late. My Son's patience will not last forever. Help me hold back **His anger, which is about to descend on sinful and ungrateful men. Suffering and anguish, such as never before experienced, is about to overtake mankind. It is the darkest hour…Hurry, my Son,** for **the time is short but the punishment will be long, and for many, will last forever.**"*

Again, Our Lady is warning us, that God is angry. In the 1950s, people were much more religious, devout and caring. There is an expression, "you ain't seen nothing yet", could accurately describe the depravity of humanity in the 1950s, to how much more perverse we have become since the 1950s. If God was upset with us then, imagine how more enraged he must be by now. Instead of a minor 'spanking' for humanity, it is going to be an all-out beating.

Matous Lasuta was a wood cutter and on June 27, 1958, Our Lady appeared to him. He was made to see the great punishment befalling upon the world if mankind does not return to God. The descriptions of the chastisements were made known to the seer. The sun will cease to warm. There will be cold summers with poor harvests. There will be terrible floods, and other misfortunes through the elements. There will be earthquakes, and mountains will move. Churches will collapse and houses will be carried away by the floods. Non-believers will blaspheme God in their despair, and the air will be filled with demon-like forms, which are the incorporations of sin and vice. These phantoms will terrify humanity Our Lady had said, *"These days will start with rolling thunder and trembling of the Earth."*

Our Lady likewise told him, *"After the **great punishment**, nature will calm down and a bright light will appear; but the **world will not be recognizable. Everything will be destroyed. It will be difficult to***

Boiling Point 2017

find life and living beings. God will punish the wicked and those who will have blasphemed Him". What will happen to the good, asked Matous? Our Lady replied, *"All my children will receive and carry the sign of the cross on their foreheads. This sign only my chosen ones will see. These chosen ones will be instructed by my angels how to conduct themselves.* **My faithful will be without any kind of fear during the most difficult hours.** *They will be protected by the good spirits and will be fed by Heaven from where they will receive further instructions. They will fall into a deathlike sleep, but they will be protected by angels. When they awake they will be like those newly born. Their bodies will be beautiful and their souls will be steeped in God. The Earth will be beautiful and my chosen ones will see how God takes care of them."*

These warnings coincide with those given to the other visionaries. It is as if it were an affirmation of not only her presence, but of humanities ruin. At the time of this deterioration, the world will be demolished, only the faithful will be protected and saved by the angels of God. Certainly in the past ten years, the world has experienced much suffering through the elements with droughts, floods, earthquakes, etc. This is only the beginning of what is about to come. Each day all we need to do to believe in her messages is to watch the negative events taking place in our world, and see how quickly mankind's destruction is approaching.

1960s

During the 1960s, there were forty-three reported visions of the Virgin Mary with sixteen of them being in Italy. The 1960s was time when many people were beginning to question their beliefs and devotion to God.

In the village of San Sebastian de Garabandal in Cantabria; four young schoolgirls Mari Loli Mazón, Jacinta González, Mari Cruz González and Conchita González had apparitions of the Blessed Virgin Mary. She appeared to them from the years 1961 to 1965 and the visitations numbered in the thousands. One of Our Lady's messages was, *"As my Message of the 18th of October has not been complied with, and as it has not been made known to the world, I am telling you that this is the last one.* **Previously, the cup was filling; now, it is brimming over. Many priests are following the road to perdition**, *and with them they are taking many more souls. Ever less* importance is being given to the Holy Eucharist. We should turn the wrath of God away from us by our own efforts... **You are now being given the last warnings...**"

Once more, the Blessed Mother was foretelling that God's priest had been compromised, and Satan was leading many into damnation. Are these the priests spoken of by Jesus in Luke's parable (13:22–27), in which Jesus said, *"Strive to enter through the narrow gate, for many, I say to you, will seek to enter and will not be able. When once the master of the house has risen up and shut the door, and you begin to stand outside and knock at the door, saying, Lord, Lord, open for us,' and he will answer and say to you, "I do not know you, where you are from,' then you will begin to say, "We ate and drank in your presence, and you taught in our streets.' But he will say, "I tell you I do not know you, where you are from. Depart from me, all you workers of iniquity."*

Besides the messages, the visionaries were told of a 'warning', a 'miracle' and a 'punishment' would follow if people do not convert and live according to the ways of God. The warning is described as a momentary stoppage of time around the world, and people see the spiritual condition of their souls, and how they should amend their ways. Within a year of the warning, a miracle will take place. The miracle will leave a permanent sign in Garabandal that can be seen and photographed.

On Good Friday in 1961, Sister Elena Aiello of Consenza, Italy received this message from the Virgin Mary, **"People pay no attention to my motherly warnings, and thus the world is falling headlong evermore into an abyss of iniquity.** *Nations shall be convulsed by terrible disasters, causing destruction and death.* **Russia, spurred on by Satan, will seek to dominate the whole world and, by bloody revolutions**, *will propagate her false teachings throughout all the nations, especially in Italy. The Church will be persecuted and the pope and the priests shall suffer much."* Sister Elena Aiello then said, "Oh, what a horrible vision I see! A great revolution is going on in Rome! They are entering the Vatican. The pope is all alone, he is praying. They are holding the pope. They have taken him by force. They knock him down to the floor and are tying him up. Oh God! Oh, God! They are kicking him. What a horrible scene! How dreadful... Flagstaffs (flying the Red flag over St. Peter's dome and elsewhere) collapse and power is gone out of the clubs of those evil brutes. These atheists are ever shouting "We don't want God to rule over us; we want Satan to be our master!" The Blessed Mother replied, *"My daughter, Rome will not be saved, because the Italian rulers have forsaken the Divine Light and because only a few people really love the church. But the day is not far off when all the wicked shall perish, under the tremendous blows of Divine Justice."*

The Virgin Mary stressed that Rome is not going to be saved from carnage, which may be attributed to the fact that only <33% of all Italians go to church, the very country in which the Vatican and the Catholic Church formed. There have been several quotations, by visionaries, of Rome being in half-ruins, and the pope having to abandon the Vatican with the bishops. In this vision, Russia which has always been against the church will found its' way to Rome and place its flag over St Peter's Basilica, as if it were a prize, not only for all the precious riches it contains, but also as a prize for those who do not believe in God.

In 1966, the Virgin Mary appeared to a farmer named Enzo Alocci, who lived in Port San Stefano, Italy. He received over eighty messages from her and Jesus. One of the messages he received by the Virgin Mary was *"The souls who have earned my goodness will be surrounded by legions of angels and the innocent will be raised to Heaven under the mantle of my Mother, while the wicked will be crushed by Me…luxury vanity and bring the world many penalties…* **volcanic phenomena** *that scientists call it,* **will erupt** *and the Earth will be covered with* **molten lava and buried towns, cities and nations.** *The persecutors of the church will be destroyed during* **three days of darkness.** *The world will be crowned with corpses and many nations will disappear from the face of the Earth. It will be great tribulation for all. Nothing will be visible to humans. The air is foul and will cause much damage and there will be a universal darkness.* **Only a quarter of humanity will survive.***"*

It was only forty years ago when this message was given, and in it were warnings of destructive volcanic eruptions. Since that time, there have been a disproportionate number of volcanic eruptions, perhaps as a prelude of what is to come, and scientists have been carefully monitoring the activity of super volcanoes. Are the super volcanoes about to erupt? If they do, most of humanity will be destroyed, and the world would not be fit for man or beast to live in. Food and water would be scarce and most of technology would be lost. Life would resemble much what it was during the days of the caveman.

Visions of the Virgin Mary of different sorts were seen in Egypt. In April of 1968, shortly after the Six-Day War with Israel, the Blessed Virgin Mary appeared for more than a year in Zeitoun, Egypt. She was seen, as an apparition on top of the dome of a Coptic Orthodox Church, by millions of people of all faiths, races, and beliefs. The apparitions lasted from only a few minutes, up to several hours. At times, she was accompanied by luminous heavenly bodies shaped like doves moving at high speeds. All of these things were photographed, and even televised by the local Egyptians. The Virgin Mary appeared sometimes in full form, and sometimes in a bust, surrounded with a halo of shining light. She was seen at times walking upon the domes on the roof of the church, and at other times floating above the domes. When she knelt in reverence in front of the cross, the cross shone with bright light. A thorough investigation was conducted, by the Egyptian government, who were looking for devices that would project the images, but nothing was found.

There were no messages given to the world other than her presence, a message to inform mankind that she exists, so does God and Jesus. Her presence was also a message to mankind that evil exists as well, and that she was there to direct mankind back to God.

The Arabic translation of El-Zeitoun means olive, and when Jesus Christ entered Jerusalem, he was welcomed by the crowds carrying olive branches and shouting, "Hosanna, Blessed is the King of Israel that cometh in the name of the Lord." Olive branches therefore symbolize salvation and peace. The Virgin Mary wanted peace and salvation to spread throughout the world, especially between the Muslims, Christians, and the Jewish peoples; most especially at this time.

1970s

In the 1970s, the number of visions decreased to thirty-four reported sightings, and it was in the 1970s, the world was beginning to change at a frantic pace. Church attendance was beginning to wane even further and people were placing more and more priorities over God. Drug usage was becoming more prevalent and available to a younger audience of teenagers. Drugs and drug dealers would seduce whole generations of children by having them focused on being 'high' rather than worshipping God. Their new lifestyle and behaviors would change America forever.

On July 6, 1973, in Akita, Japan, Sr. Agnes Sasagawa had several visions of the Blessed Virgin Mary, who conveyed this message to her, *"...Many men in this world afflict the Lord... In order that the world might know his anger, the heavenly father will **inflict a terrible punishment** on all humanity. It will be **a punishment greater than the deluge**, such as one will never have seen before... The **survivors will** find themselves so desolate that they will **envy the dead**."*

A month later Mary reiterated, *"In order that the world might know His anger, **the heavenly Father is preparing to inflict a great chastisement on all** mankind. I have intervened so many times to appease the wrath of the Father. I have prevented the coming of calamities by offering Him the sufferings of the Son on the cross, His precious blood, and beloved souls who console Him forming..."*

In 1973, Mother Elena Leonardi, who been under the guidance of Padre Pio received a vision of God, Jesus, and Mary. It was the Virgin Mary, who had given her this message *"This will be **a time of despair for the impious**: with shouts and satanic blasphemy, **they will beg to be covered by the mountains**, and they will try to seek refuge in caverns, but to no avail...**Russia will be almost completely burned**."*

The Virgin Mary has given numerous warnings about the amount of evil Russia will introduce into the world. In her message to Elena, it will be Russia that will be punished for all the crimes it has committed towards mankind, throughout the world. Russia will burn.

The messages given to Sister Agnes Sasagawa and Mother Elena Leonardi, about chastisements resemble a broken record stuck on the same track, in which one hears the words over and over again. However, if something is to be credible, it has to be heard from a multitude of sources to believable. Her allusion to survivors envying the dead, parallels the passage from Revelation (6:15–17), *"The kings of the Earth, the nobles, the military officers, the rich, the powerful, and every slave and free persons hid themselves in caves, and among the mountain crags. They cried out to the mountains and rocks, fall on us and hid us from the one who sits on the throne and from the wrath of the lamb. Because the great day of the Lord has come and who can withstand it?"*

Fr. Stefano Gobbi received interior locutions from the Blessed Virgin Mary. Although he did not see her, he heard her voice say in July 28, 1973, *"The time of apostasy---the **great loss of faith** emphasized at Fatima and mentioned long before by Paul in his Second Letter to the Thessalonians---was unfolding."* During this era, attendance at church continued to decrease, both in America and in strongholds such as France, where she'd made such an effort through apparitions.

The Virgin Mary further stated, **"Priests were being seduced or discouraged by Satan**...*and sin was justified and even extolled by academics, movie makers, and the media*... *"Many Christians have been made a 'sport' by Satan, complained the Virgin*... Such an hour is the hour *"when **the abomination of desolation is truly entering into the holy temple** of God"*.

And on October 24, 1975, Mary told him, *"My angels have already begun the battle, at my order they are bringing these sons of mine together from all parts of the world."* It was the crucial role of these priests *to 'live only for my Son Jesus, carrying out the Gospel to the letter',* which would enable them to outweigh the faithless priests **"who no longer believe** *and yet they still remain in my Church, true wolves in sheep's clothing."*

Night had now fallen upon the world, Mary lamented to Gobbi. It was the time of Satan's greatest triumph. There were even people attacking the purity of Jesus– *"such a horrible and satanic blasphemy that all Heaven is, as it were, dismayed and incredulous!"* For that and other reasons, *"a tremendous and now inevitable storm"* was about to break upon humanity; the **"demon of corruption, the spirit of lust, has seduced all the nations of the world!** *Not one of them is any longer preserved."*

Fr. Stefano's messages from the Virgin Mary reflects the times that Jesus denoted as the sign proceeding the great tribulation, written in Matthew (24:15), *"When you see the desolating abomination spoken of through Daniel the prophet standing in the holy place (let the reader understand), then those in Judea must flee to the mountains... woe to pregnant women and nursing in those days... for at that time will be the great tribulation."* It is understood, this message is a prelude to the antichrist's coming, at the moment when people have abandoned their faith and follow Satan instead.

In 1974, in the city of Dozule, France, a woman named Madeleine Aumont had a vision of Jesus Christ, who gave her this message, *"... You are living the time of the supreme effort of evil against the Christ.* **Satan is unleashed from his prison***, and occupies the face of the Earth... Tell the church to renew its message of peace to the entire world, for the hour is grave.* **Satan is seducing minds***, and rendering them capable of destroying humanity. If humanity does not oppose him, I will allow him to act and it will be a catastrophe... and this before the end of the century. All who will have come to repent at the foot of the 'Glorious Cross' will be saved. Satan will be destroyed, only peace and joy will remain... If man does not rise up the cross I will make it appear, but there will be no more time left... After these days of distress, the* **Son of Man himself will appear in the heavens** *with great majesty and great power, to gather together the elect from the four corners of the Earth... In truth I tell you, the heavens and Earth will pass but my words will not...* **do not lament over the general cataclysm of this generation***, for all this must come to pass. But behold what is appearing in the sky, the sign of the Son of Man..."*

Each and every day atrocities are committed throughout the world and are recognized as works of evil, thus this message given to Madeleine Aumont by Jesus clearly ascertains we are living in those sadistic days. Satan has been released from his prison; the consequences being that we have remained deluded by his power and are openly rebelling against God. Jesus, himself, made it known to Madeleine Aumont that we are living in the last times, and He would be coming back to the world from the heavens. This was confirmed in the Book of Acts (1:10) *"While they were looking intently at the sky as he was going, suddenly two men dressed in white stood beside them. They said, men of Galilee, why are you looking at the sky? This Jesus who has been taken up from you into Heaven will return the same way as you have seen him going into Heaven."* Therefore, Jesus's return is imminent and soon He will ascend from the sky as a warrior, who will conquer Satan.

Chapter 17

Visions (The Water Is Getting Hot: 1980-2000s)

1980s

Between the 1980s and 2000s there have been more than one-hundred-thirty reported visions of the Blessed Virgin Mary. In the 1980s there were an unprecedented number of Marian apparitions, with ninety-four individuals seeing the Virgin Mary and thousands of messages for the world. She was actively seen in every continent in the world, and has been pressing humanity to heed her warnings. The 1980s was a changing time in technology, moral values, and there was preponderance for greed unlike that ever seen before. It was the beginning of very ominous times for the country, and for the world. Indeed, the world was on a pinnacle of a transformation that would further enhance Satan's reign over humanity. Visionaries throughout the world were calling for mankind to return to God, or suffer the consequences of their choices.

In 1982, the Blessed Virgin Mary appeared in Rwanda, Africa to a young teenager named Marie-Clare Mukangango, who at that time was an atheist. The Blessed Mother gave her this message *"the world is in revolt against God, and the* **world is on the edge of catastrophe**.*"* It was a life altering experience for Marie-Clare to see and hear the words of the Blessed Virgin Mary.

More messages of mankind's impending hour of doom were given in a small village in Betania, Venezuela to a woman named Maria Esperanza, who asserted to have seen the Virgin Mary. Maria was told that **Jesus is on the verge of a major appearance upon the Earth.** Her vision of the Virgin Mary and message in June, 1987 was *"Children, the hour is soon approaching..."* In 1988, the Virgin Mary's message was *"Daughter, children, here among you, in a close and warm embrace... since Jesus My Divine Son, with His word of wisdom, with his righteousness and His immutable purity, is longing to continue to serve and to be useful to His people... He is **not coming to gather only the good, but it is the rebellious** whom He comes to gather, to have them drink from the fountain of the 'Holy Waters' of this mother, so they can wash their heads, their hands and their feet, for their conversion..! Children, I beg all of you to **take advantage of the days, hours, minutes, and seconds, to prepare yourselves...!"*

The Blessed Virgin Mary is informing us to prepare for the final judgment, for it will soon be upon us. Jesus is gathering the good, as well as those sinners, who entrust themselves to Him and turn away from their sins. The Virgin Mary's description for the amount of time left being in; days, hours, minutes and seconds, emphasizes humanity is close to the period of tribulation. How many times do we need to hear her plea for conversion, before it becomes too late?

In 1987, an additional urgent message for the world and of its ultimate demise was given to Brother David Lopez, by the Blessed Virgin Mary. She told him, *"**Do not be afraid about the three days of darkness that will come over the Earth**, because those who are living my messages and have a life of interior prayer will be alerted by an interior voice three days to one week before their occurrence. My children must continue with repentance for their sins and pray more as I have recommended. They should get holy water, and blessed articles, and have a special devotion to the Sacred Heart of Jesus, having always a vigil light in front of him. **Before the great tribulation**, there is going to be a sign. We will see in the sky one **great 'Red Cross'** on a day of blue sky without clouds. The color red signifies the blood of Jesus who redeemed us and the blood of the martyrs selected by God in the days of darkness. This cross will be seen by everyone: Christians, pagans, atheists, etc., as well as all the prepared ones.*

It was understood by Brother David Lopez that there would be impending signs before these three days of darkness. These signs would consists of increasing violent disturbances; such as, earthquakes, hurricanes, tornadoes, windstorms, cloudbursts, dams collapsing, rivers overflowing, huge tidal waves, floods, famines, epidemics, destruction, destitution, failure of crops, and pollution of potable water. There would be revolutions, downfall of governments, dissensions, wars, confusion in high places, lack of respect for authority, treachery, corruption, brutalities, and atrocities. It will be a time for the breakdown of family life, immortality, adultery, infidelity, promiscuity, perversion and violence of youth, disobedience, lack of values, indecent nakedness of dress, countless sins and iniquities, people concerned only with eating, drinking, dancing, and pleasures.

These imminent signs of tragedy and upheaval are in fact being, or have been fulfilled. The number of hours, minutes, or seconds we have left in our world before the sign appears, are becoming fewer each day.

Pedro Régis Alves of Anguera – Barcelona, Spain was another visionary who received messages from the Virgin Mary about an upcoming darkness. She told him, *"Soon there will be **three consecutive days of darkness, which is not able to explain science. These are days of great suffering**. I promise everyone that is on my side that the light will not fail them. I beseech you that ye blessed candles always home for priests."*

The Virgin Mary similarly told Marcos Tadeu Teixeira of Jacareí, Spain, *"**The three days of darkness will come soon after the fall of the antichrist**. It will be the last stand of the enemy, his last attempt to destroy the man. But at the dawn of the third day he will be totally defeated by the 'Virgin' and Saint Michael. The Earth then ceases to tremble…**But before you place a lot of pain, many earthquakes, the moon will burn in blood,** return to their volcanoes eruptions, stars fall from heaven…"*

In 1991, seer Christina Gallagher of Mythic Ireland received this message from Mary, *"It is time for purification of humanity. A **great darkness will cover the world**. The heavens tremble. The thunder and lightning shine like never before. My hand will fall on the world faster than the wind…"*

In 1988, the Visionary Patricia Talbot of Ecuador, said the Blessed Mother told her, *"**The Earth will leave its orbit for three days**. … In those days, families should keep in constant prayer. …**During these three days of darkness**, we should not open the door of the house to anyone, but just continue praying.* The Blessed Mother also said, *"It is best not to look through the windows, not to see the righteousness of God falling on the people."

In 1983, Luz Cuevas Amapari - Escorial was given a vision, and saw **land covered in thick darkness for three days and three nights**. Nothing can be seen. The air is noxious and poisonous. The only light will come from blessed candles that will burn for three days. The enemies of the church across the face of the Earth will die, with the exception of a few. There will be rain of fire, and the entire Earth will tremble. **Rome will be destroyed,** the **Vatican will disappear**! Ultimately, peace will reign on Earth.

Many visionaries have all had the same vision of darkness prior to the time of misfortunes. Perhaps the darkness represents all of those demons, who had been let out of Hell, and are allowed to torment those who have not converted. These demons may drive some people mad while other persons may even try to kill themselves at this time. This period of darkness may also be much like the time when the Jews marked their doorpost with blood to protect their firstborn from the angel of death. They were told to stay inside to be protected from this reaper. Similarly, during the upcoming days of darkness, the Virgin Mary warns us not to go outside or even look outside; perhaps if we do, we will be like Lot's wife who looked back at the city of Sodom, longing for that lifestyle in her heart. She was not saved from death.

In 1983, at the home of Gladys Quiroga de Motta, who lives in San Nicolas de los Arroyos, Argentina, the Virgin Mary appeared to Gladys and informed her, *"At the present time, all mankind is pending by a thread. If that thread is broken, many will be lost for those that do not have salvation. For that reason, I call you to reflect upon your lives, hurry up, you are running out of time; there will be no place for late comers...* **The coming of the Lord is imminent**, *and as written in the scriptures nobody knows the day or the hour it will be; and certainly for that hour the soul of the Christian must be prepared. Even the stones will know of him."*

In 1984, Mr William Kamm of Nowra, New South Wales, Australia apparently received this message from the Virgin Mary, *"The world is fast coming to a great war, one that will end all wars."*

Estela Ruiz has apparitions and receives messages from our Blessed Mother, who calls herself Our Lady of the America. Since

1988, she has given messages for all the people in the world. In 1990, Our Lady said, *"I come to **warn you**, my little ones, that the world is at a crossroad… It will either cross into the path of destruction, or allow Our Lord to reign in the hearts of men. **Time is running short**. I am here to beg all who listen to turn to God. **The signs of the times tell you that the world is in crisis**. **The greatest offense against God is the lack of respect for life.** Yes, that is the greatest offense going on in the world. **Never before has man destroyed life** so much as during these times. **This is done cruelly and without conscience.**"* And in 1994, she said, *"My Dear Children, **Satan and his demons have overtaken this world** and pain, overwhelming pain is the result. Satan brings death…not only of the body, as he moves many to bring death to others, but more importantly the death of your souls.… **He brings envy, lust, jealousy, mistrust, hate and anger and all this destroys the soul**. The more he pulls you into these ways, the weaker you become until one day, you become part of the walking dead, moving around at Satan's will, helping him to destroy others."*

In 1995, Our Lady related to her, *"**Evil has been loosened all over the world… He no longer hides but is out openly visible.** Many do not recognize him because their hearts are covered by the world's ways… **the heavens weep as the world moves ever closer to destruction and war**… Humanity has allowed the evil of Satan to overpower it and his power is rampant over the whole of mankind. **Chaos, destruction, hate, and greed abound.**"* In other messages she conveyed to her, *"This is the beginning of a great crisis that will occur. "You cannot begin to understand the spiritual warfare that is going on… **Satan has unleashed all the demons in Hell**…We will not win this war without **disasters and catastrophes** because the evil one is powerful and has many who follow him." "I come to warn you, my little ones, that the world is at a crossroad. It will either cross into the path of destruction, or allow Our Lord to reign in the hearts of men. **Time is running short**."*

The messages given to Estela are an affirmation that Satan and his legions of demons have been freed from the pit of hell. They are creating chaos and leading the world into destruction. Acts of disrespect for life being the greatest offense to God could be referring to the number of abortions committed daily in our world. She pointed out the Satan is no longer hiding, and this is evident just by watching the news or reading the newspapers. He is bold and arrogant because people do not believe he exits. He no longer has to operate under cover, but instead he operates in the wide open with impunity. The Virgin Mary has said that Satan knows that his time is coming to an end, and therefore has let all the stops out. Homosexuality, murder, greed, hatred, lust, envy etc. are inundating our world, a world that lacks in faith.

Patricia Talbott Borrero (Pachi), a seer from Ecuador of Cuenca has reportedly seen the Blessed Virgin Mary more than one hundred times since 1988. According to Pachi, the Virgin Mary acknowledged that minor chastisements had been adverted through prayer, but a major chastisement still looms in the future due to the deteriorating moral situation in the world. From the early 1990s, Pachi has warned us that our descent into sexual immorality, godlessness, and materialism could lead to a nuclear event, a war in Eurasia, and natural disasters created by man.

Our Lady presented herself to a dozen teenagers in Oliveto Citra, Italy between the years 1985-1989. She was called Our Lady of Graces. In 1988, she divulged to them, *"...when God comes among you with some manifestation,* **He does not come as a joke**. *He does not joke and He is not afraid of men, so take this message seriously... Peace on Earth is about to end, the world cannot be saved without peace...,* but the **world will find peace only if mankind returns to God**. *I will engage in the final struggle against Satan which will conclude with the triumph of my immaculate heart... Those who refuse God today will go far from Him tomorrow... The whole world is in danger.* **There will be earthquakes, famines, and punishments for all the inhabitants of Earth**..."

Eileen George reported that she had visions of Jesus Christ in 1982. He conveyed to her, *"There will be a World War III and it will be started by a man who wears the turban of the faith, a Muslim. He will be an antichrist put on Earth by Lucifer. Yet there is a more powerful one to rise in Syria, when this one has accomplished his work. He will cause destruction and pain. He will cause heartache and tears and great persecution of Christians. The Earth will tremble with earthquakes. He will be a great ruler of Satan, after many years of battle."* She seemed to indicate the battle would last fifteen years and this antichrist will be connected to the communists. He will wear a long robe, be very intelligent, and be well-equipped for war. He is going to be worse than Hitler and will fire rockets at us.

The message given to Eileen by Jesus indicates there will be a Muslim-Christian war, and it will precipitate World War III. In the early 1980, most Muslim countries did not have the means to sustain a war, but now Iran is attempting to acquire nuclear weaponry with the aid of the Russians. Iranian President Mahmoud Ahmadinejad has a black mustache and very well may be the antichrist spoken of. He has ambitions to destroy Israel and the United States with aid from Russia, a country the Virgin Mary has continually warned us about. In the future, he may be capable of sending nuclear weapons towards both countries.

1990s

In the 1990s many countries were at war with an evil dictator named Saddam Hussein. It was the beginning of a war in the Middle East that has spread to neighboring countries like Afghanistan. The amount of hatred towards the West is growing, and mankind still has more faith in the dollar than in God. The 1990s were a transforming period for humankind, and each year grew sequentially worse throughout the decade.

In 1970, Veronica Lueken, a seer from Bayside, New York began receiving messages from the Virgin Mary, but in 1994, she received this message from Jesus, *"You will continue, my children, with the prayers of atonement. And I must tell you the time is, in* **Earth time, growing short.** *There will be* **a great 'Chastisement' sent upon mankind**. *You will recognize this* **when you find out in the atmosphere a huge, immense ball of light**. *Do not be affrighted, my child. Your scientists will be bewildered. It is the little people who know the truth."*

Jesus's allusion to a great ball a light in the sky is synonymous to messages given to other visionaries, along with Nostradamus, Mother Shipton, and Edgar Cayce all of whom predicted that something was going to fall out of the sky from the east. This will set off time of the great chastisement. Jesus told her that scientist will not be able to explain this light. It will come out of nowhere; possibly it is currently being hidden from our view behind the sun or other planetary objects, or maybe it will be divinely created and appear out of nothingness.

In 1992, two women named Veronica Garcia and Theresa Lopez from Denver, Colorado had locutions of the Virgin Mary.

Mary told of future events and about the coming of a **permanent sign in the sky**, which everyone will see. It will be proof that she had been here on Earth. They were also told of the importance for conversion of mankind before the sign comes; otherwise it will be too late. After the sign will come a miracle; one that displays the presence of God, and shortly after the miracle, the chastisements will follow. The Virgin said the good people will have their focus on Heaven and won't have despair, worry, fright or any other human emotions. For those who did not choose to convert, they will retain their sins and earthly views because they will be of the Earth. They on the other hand will feel the despair and the agony of the chastisements". Our Lady iterated to her, *"Those who live a virtuous life have no fear of chastisements. After all these chastisements come to pass, even then, there will be one hour of grace remaining. And in that hour of grace, even the worst of the worst that have undergone the chastisements will be given the last opportunity for conversion.* **The New Jerusalem will then settle upon Earth.** *All evil will no longer exist and we will be in perpetual paradise, just as God planned in the beginning."*

Another message given to Veronica Garcia by the Virgin Mary was *"Time is running out my small ones, the chastisements have begun. It will only be those who have accepted this invitation of 'life' that will be saved from certain ruin".*

Both of these locutionists' messages are focused upon the end times, which are within reach of our existence. The description of a New Jerusalem settling upon the Earth mirrors that which is written in Revelation (21:9), where there is the establishment of a New Jerusalem and new Earth, once the world is destroyed.

In December of 1998, Patricia Mundorf was given by the Virgin Mary, a futuristic vision of America. She could see that it was in the springtime because of the cherry blossoms in Washington, D.C. She saw New York City being swallowed up by an enormous wave, which was engulfing the whole city. The Statue of Liberty had been bent at an angle as result of the wave and all of New York City, Long Island, and most of New Jersey were under water. She said, "I was given the understanding that around this time, there are major cataclysms elsewhere. Volcanic eruptions in the northwestern portion of the United States, starts a chain of earthquakes that will reach all the way down to California. I was shown the Golden Gate Bridge, which will be crushed by a tsunami, except for the

Boiling Point 2017

northern (Marin County) end. Most all of California will be in ruins." Patricia saw the destruction of the United States extending all the way to Canada. In the north-central part of the country, the Dakotas were under water, as was most of the country. The remnants of land left resembled islands rather than a country. She was shown a large object hitting the Earth, which originated from space, and was given to understand it caused the waves that destroyed the Eastern USA seaboard and heavily damaging the Statue of Liberty.

Patricia is not the only visionary who was shown of an unknown large object hitting Earth. This is a recurring theme, and from Patricia's description of the destruction in California and New York experiencing tsunamis; indicates this massive object will break into pieces, hitting both major oceans and cause worldwide destruction. This picture of events has been mentioned by other visionaries as well.

In 1999, a message was given to Gianna Talone Sullivan, by the Mother of God, was "*Evil has struck the Earth and* **spirits of darkness are everywhere leading people astray**. **Many are abandoning the faith**. *Even priests are breaking away from the True Word of God. God needs children of his light and children too of his merciful love. Do not fall into Satan's trap.*"

This common theme of the abandonment of faith 'the apostasy' has been reiterated in prior messages. It is like the key, which when put into the lock, opens it. Similarly, the abandonment of faith is the key that opens the doors to chastisements. How could a good and just God continue to give gifts to unappreciative and unbelieving lot of people? These unfaithful thankless people are like children born from a family of wealth and they end-up receiving riches not earned by them. Because they didn't sacrifice, their behavior frequently becomes out-of-control and consequentially they treat others with contempt and disrespect. Yet, they still expect to inherit their parents' wealth. Why would any parent give their wealth to children showing no gratitude? In the same respect, why would God give anything to those who have abandoned and disrespected him?

In 1993, an older man named Ray Doiron of Bellville, Illinois had numerous visions and messages from the Blessed mother. Her messages consisted of trials for mankind and this is what she conveyed, "Behold I have told you **great trials shall befall mankind**, and many of these catastrophes have occurred. They are allowed by God to awaken you from slumber of your soul. For I solemnly assure you **God's justice shall destroy your entire material world,** which has become your God. You let material things enslave you and you worship them as false idols. **The great battle rages,** but you refuse to see or recognize it." She said," We are in a great troubled time now. Do you think that the earthquake in Japan, the **great floods, intense drought, and heat** we are having now in the eastern and southern states in the U.S. are just a happening? These are **signs from Heaven to change your ways here on Earth**, and the only way is total conversion of heart to God and through prayer; prayer is the only answer." **John** came and **proclaimed the coming of the Messiah**. "He was a voice crying out in the desert, and people then refused to hear him. I come to tell you to make way and prepare the straight path for the Lord, just as John did. **I am the herald crying out to the Second Coming**. This is why, as no other time in history, Heaven has opened up to its people to give messages and apparitions from me and signs from Heaven as never before."

Mary is clearing the way for her son Jesus's return to Earth; just as John the Baptist did for Jesus, two thousand years ago. However he will not be returning as a meek and mild person, but as a conqueror over those who had partaken in malevolent practices, and adopted the ways of Satan. Mary is telling us that, no matter how much material wealth one has, no matter how much fame one has, no matter how much power one has, they are worthless. They will be swept away as garbage at the Second Coming of Jesus Christ.

Nancy Fowler, a woman from Conyers, Georgia, has reportedly received numerous messages from the Virgin Mary and Jesus from 1991 until 1998. In 1992, the Virgin Mary told her, "*I am the Immaculate Conception. I am the spouse of the Holy Spirit. Behold a new Pentecost is coming. A* **new Heaven** *and* **a new Earth is dawning, but first the old will be destroyed**. *Fire will fall down from Heaven. Lightning will flash from one end of the sky to the other and the* **Earth will plunge into a darkness it has never seen**. *The world has chosen these punishments.*" In 1992, she told Nancy, "*The time will come when all mankind will see their sins. This is a time of grace. It is a great grace from God. Some of my children will experience intense heat. It is a healing.*"

Later in 1992, Jesus included, **"Darkness will fall over the whole world and stars will fall."** and *"The day will come when fire will fall from heaven."* While praying, Nancy saw a vision of great, tremendous waves hitting the shores of a city she understood to be in the United States. In 1994, Jesus said, *"My children, you have ignored God long enough. Woe be to the inhabitants of the Earth. With a mighty blow* **I will pound the Earth, earthquake after earthquake, volcanoes will erupt, tidal waves,** *famine. The water will become polluted in many places. Diseases, every kind of affliction awaits this sinful generation. You choose to sin of your own free will, then with your own free will you will suffer."*

A message in 1994, from our Blessed Mother to Nancy was *"The greatest suffering is about to befall mankind. Children, my dear children, prepare now. The time has come for God to punish all mankind. Pray, fast, little ones. Please. The events I speak about are close at hand. Remain faithful! All of you should have blessed candles, a blessed image of my Son and holy water in your homes."*

Also in 1994, Jesus communicated this message to Nancy *"The clock continues to tick.* **The hour is rapidly approaching when one disaster after another will befall you.** *There will be fighting everywhere. There will be famine and polluted water in many places. Great waves will crash upon your shores and you will experience cold when you should experience warmth.* **Flood waters will increase in many places.** *Fire will be upon the Earth. You will think that the heavens and the Earth have rebelled against you. The clock continues to tick…"*

The messages given to her by both Jesus and Mary are ones focused upon urgency. They are messages indicating humanity does not have much time, and the alarm clock is about to go off. When it does, there will be massive destruction in the United States and upon the Earth as a whole. Her message also re-iterated an object will fall from the sky; afterwards, there will be volcanic eruptions and a multitude of earthquakes. Warning after warning of impending dangers has been given to the visionaries. An incalculable number of messages have been given of flood waters increasing in many places of the world and in the central portion of the United States during the year of 2011. Disasters after disasters have been taking place throughout the world in the past decade. Are these signs that the hour of Jesus is rapidly coming closer?

In 1992, a message was given to the respected visionary and stigmatic, Father Gobbi, by the Blessed Virgin Mary. She said, **"Each man will see himself in the blazing fire of the divine truth**. *It will be like the judgment but in a smaller scale... what will occur will be something so grand that it will surpass every event that has happened since the beginning of the world. It will be like a small judgment and each individual will see their own life and everything that they have done, in the same light of God."* A message given to him by Jesus in the same year was *"My children, I cannot wait any longer. It is unbearable to watch the evil that has invaded your world, the abuses of the innocents and their families. You all will remember that I* **granted Lucifer 100 years to do its worst to win the souls of the children of God. Those 100 years have come to its end** *and the destruction of the souls has been tremendous. But I still have two wars pending for the souls. These will be battles of great magnitude. The remnant church will persevere for God; it will be declared itself for God in the Blessed Trinity. The first battle will be the* 'Great Warning' *produced by the great love of our Blessed Virgin Mary for you. This will forewarn all of humanity, to the people everywhere, to the people of all races and tongues in regards to their souls. This is war because the evil spirits are also waiting for this day. They too have a plan in which they will do everything possible to provoke desperation and disgrace to the faithful. Their plan is to scare, to instill fear to the souls, to make them hesitant to follow the right road. They will seduce, cajole and slander those who do not return to their wicked ways. They will mock those who persevere in prayer. They will do these things because they know that the people are willing to listen and return to their old habits. The evil spirits will encourage them to do it because they will tell them that everything that has occurred is a test from their leader. Because he directs the evil forces that all will see and feel.* **It will be a war to get your souls**, *my dear children.* **Shortly after this event, the second battle will take place**. *This will be the* 'Great Miracle' *during which you should declare yourself for God."*

This message continually emphasizes that we are in the last times, and are in a spiritual war, this unseen war will claim many lives. The true believers will be attacked by the demons, who are attempting to break their faith in God. Those who leave their faith may find themselves being counted, as the lost souls. It is imperative that believers hold on during the worse of the worst of times and believe. All those bad things being experienced are due to Satan, who is attempting to break their wills at the most critical time in one's religious devotion. Jesus tells us to hold on and endure until the 'Great Miracle'.

2000s

The 2000s began a time when war still waging in Iraq and shortly afterwards, extended into Afghanistan. Religious zealots like Osama Bin Laden were rallying many extremist, and declared a 'holy war' upon the western cultures. This holy war killed thousands of innocent people.

The world has become an unsafe place for many people, and their lure of wealth, fame, power and greed continued, without any regard for the less fortunate. It is a time when God's clock to end the world is about to strike the midnight hour.

On December 24, 2004, the Blessed Virgin Mary relayed this message to Julián Soto of Ayala, Mexico, *"The world that you have received for inheritance awaits eagerly its regeneration. The time begins in which each soul will account before God its own life through the abundance of grace that will be bestowed upon the world; the time begins for the maximum test, in which all will see the greatest miracle of the world, by which all will be purified. One suffering after another; it is only the beginning of the pains.* **You cannot, dear children, imagine how dreadful the end of history will be for all humanity**. *An arid wind will cross the deserts doing away with all life; an icy wind, frightfully cold, will burn what is left of the plant life.* **An Armageddon will assemble the nations of the Earth to fight against the 'Anointed One' and those who are faithful;** *the nations armed with the most powerful and sophisticated weapons will spread death and harvest the ruin. A total coldness of the faith will embrace all of humanity. The natural resources will be destroyed.* **A great famine will force many to turn to delinquency**; *the sky and many of the rivers will be contaminated; rare diseases will appear in Europe that will be difficult to cure. You will vomit blood from the eyes, nose and ears; and only the remedies sent by Heaven will cure those who are in the state of grace. Each day that passes will seem much longer than the previous one, because the pains of the purification will seem endless. When the situation seems hopeless the 'Great Miracle' will occur, as the final effort of Heaven to save souls."*

These messages are telling that the midnight hour is only minutes away and that the suffering to humanity will be on an unthinkable scale. The whole world is being tested, and many are failing because of their love for the things of the world. Their love for the world and lack of love for God will bring a rain of destruction upon the Earth. It will be the time when God's faithful will hold steadfast and fight against Satan.

Joseph Terelya spent twenty-three years in Soviet labor camps and prisons for committing the crime of remaining a Ukrainian Catholic. He was devoted to the Virgin Mary and during his time of imprisonment, she appeared to him. She gave him messages until the time of his death in 2009. In August of 2005, he was given this message, "*Peace be with you, my child! I have come to bring another warning to my children. The **warnings given before and many times**, have gone unheeded by most souls. Have the natural disasters and illnesses that have come upon mankind not been enough for all to open their eyes, as well as their souls? No, for the warnings are not taken seriously! However, many will experience the terrible fate that awaits many. In the **USA and Canada** there will occur **many earthquakes, hurricanes** and sicknesses…*"

Once more, the theme of natural disasters coming upon the world in the form of earthquakes, hurricanes and sickness are shortcoming; however, in this message these disasters are directed more toward North America. She is attempting to guide Americans back to their fundamental belief in God, just as the time when Puritans left their homeland to come to America for religious freedom. We are not to make money or other things of this world into our god, and if we chose not to listen, the inevitable is on the horizon.

More recent apocalyptic messages for the end times were given to Pedro Régis of Brazil, who had visions of the Blessed Virgin Mary beginning in October of 1987. Numerous messages of impending disasters in the world were given to him in the year 2009. The Virgin Mary said, "*Difficult days are coming and my poor children will experience a heavy cross. **Continents will disappear** and people will contemplate things that are not visible to the human eye now. These will be sorrowful times for you… The force of nature will provoke phenomenon never seen before. **Objects will be thrown from the Earth by a force that no one can explain**. Forces will arise from the depths of the Earth that leave men preoccupied, but I want to tell you that God will not abandon his people. Pray. You will yet see things that human eyes have* *never seen. **Rivers of fire will flow on the Earth**; the crust of the Earth will split in many regions of the Earth. **Energy coming from the interior of the Earth** will bring suffering to many of my poor children. Death will pass through Spain. Costa Rica will live moments of anguish. **A sleeping giant will bring suffering and death to Africa and Europe** will be poor and there will be great despair everywhere. **The Middle East will shake with great atomic holocaust**. Something sorrowful will happen in the house of The Lord and people will have to weep and lament. Enemies will open the doors and bearded men will act with great fury."*

The Virgin Mary has continually indicated that a great object from space is going to hit the Earth. She has told this to a great number of visionaries in every part of the world and it can be assumed that these visionaries have not communicated with one another. That being the case, then this object is real and coming our way, and when it strikes the Earth many volcanoes will erupt and the lava will cover the Earth as rivers of fire. She mentions that something sorrowful will happen in the house of the Lord and that it may be an atomic blast in Israel caused by 'bearded men' who may be either the Taliban, Al Qaeda or Iranians. All of them hate the Jews and they would love to be known, as the ones who destroy them.

On March 20, 2010 Mary told him that *"a mega-quake will shake Japan and my poor children will weep and lament."* As predicted, a year later, a massive 9.0 earthquake struck off the coast of Japan on March 11, 2011 killing thousands of men, women and children, who perished from a tsunami that swept inland.

Also in 2009, the Virgin Mary predicted, **"Humanity is heading towards a sorrowful** *future. The Earth will shake and abysses will appear. My poor children will carry a heavy cross.* **The Earth will lose its equilibrium** *and frightening phenomena will appear. Earth will lose equilibrium."*

How many visionaries and prophets have said that the Earth will lose its equilibrium? Is it a metaphor for people losing their guidance by the Holy Spirit, or are these current predictions used to substantiate those made by the Mayans, Nostradamus and Edgar Cayce? There appears to be a correlation between the Earth losing its equilibrium and all the disasters of volcanic eruptions, three days of darkness, fire in the skies etc. The question that remains is what causes the Earth to be knocked off its axis, an asteroid?

In 2010, the Virgin Mary predicted disasters in other parts of Europe, particularly in Germany. She spoke to Pedro Régis and said, "There *are some bad days heading for Europe. A devastating force will cross Europe causing destruction and death. Humanity will drink the bitter cup of suffering.* **A frightening event will happen to Iran, in Pakistan** *and in Angra dos Reis (*Brazil*). The happenings will be in different times, but will be alike. A **sleeping giant will arise in Indonesia** and my poor children will drink the bitter cup of pain".*

She speaks of frightening events that will happen in Europe, Iran, Pakistan, Indonesia, and Brazil. The sleeping giant she spoke of being located in Indonesia can be a super volcano erupting. There are sister super volcanoes in Europe as well. Are all of these events related? Will they all erupt at the same time? If so, there are many earthquake fault lines that go through Iran and Pakistan; a super volcano eruption in Indonesia could set off a series of major earthquakes in Pakistan and Iran. Since both countries have, or will have, nuclear weapons, these earthquakes could destroy their nuclear facilities, in so doing, release toxic radiation.

A more recent message given by the Virgin Mary to Mary Luz de Maria on March 19, 2010 was, **"Convert, repent, before the Warning comes** *and the weight of sin makes you suffer to the very core of your entrails, ripping your soul apart when you find out the distance that you have created from God, by the lack of love and disobedience that you have lived continually. The Earth evolves at the same speed as sin, men is marking his future.* **The attack on nature will continue to hurl down one after the other***, and they are not but the beginning of the closeness of the WARNING; this will be the mean for humanity to stop and meditate before continuing with their life."*

During first eleven years of the twenty-first century, the world has experienced an abundant number of bizarre weather incidences. There have been record amounts of heat, snow, rain, drought, earthquake activity, volcanic eruptions, etc. Each successive year, these natural phenomena have been growing at an incredible pace each year. The amount of rain is increasing, the heat is getting hotter, and the cold is getting colder. This is exactly what the Blessed Mother forewarned in this message given to Mary Luz Maria. As the advertising salesman on television would say, "wait, there's still more." We can only anticipate a cascade of bad things to come upon us.

Chapter 18

Visions (The Water Is Boiling)

The most phenomenal assemblages of Marian apparitions are appearing to six visionaries (Ivan, Marija, Ivanka, Mirjana, Jakov and Vicka) in Medjugorje, Yugoslavia. The comparison of all the visions and messages given by the Virgin Mary, throughout the twentieth century; to those given by her at Medjugorje, would be like watching fireworks going off one by one, versus a multitude of them going off in the grand finale. The Blessed Virgin Mary has been seen by at least one or more of these visionaries ever since June 24, 1981. It has been thirty years that the Virgin Mary has appeared there on a daily basis, this equates to almost twelve thousand appearances by Our Holy Mother.

Why would she appear so many times to these visionaries; unless calamitous times of biblical proportions are in the near future for the world? If the messages given by the Virgin Mary at Fatima were an indicator to the beginning of the end times; then those given at Medjugorje would mean the completion of those days. The Blessed Mother would not waste so much time in the world, unless the danger level reached at an all-time high. The world is like a steam engine's pressure gauge in the red zone. It's about ready to blow.

The visionaries were at the ages of 10, 15, and four 16-year-olds when these apparitions began and they are currently in their early to mid-forties. The Virgin Mary has not only been giving them secrets pertaining to the world, but each visionary has received personal messages. Some of the messages pertain to their private lives, but no one knows how many of the other secrets relate to the end times. The visionaries reveal very little about the things to remain hidden at this time. When they are pressed about whether the secrets pertain to the last days, they quickly redirect the discussion and say they cannot discuss them. Even if they tried to speak about some of them in detail, the Blessed Mother intervenes and prevents the visionaries from revealing this information.

However, the Virgin Mary has permitted Mirjana to reveal part of the secret. Mirjana said, "Before the visible sign is given to mankind, there will be three warnings to the world. The warnings will be in the form of events on Earth." Mirjana said that she will be a witness to them and ten days before they occur, Mirjana will notify a priest of her choice, Fr. Petar Ljubicic, who will be 65-years old in 2011. She continued, "After these admonitions, the visible sign will appear on the site of the apparitions in Medjugorje for all the people to see. The sign will be given as a testimony, confirming the apparitions and to call people back to faith." After the first warning, there will be short interval of grace for conversion. After the visible sign appears, **those who are still alive** will have little time for conversion. It is imperative for this reason, the Blessed Virgin urges us to conversion and reconciliation. The invitation to prayer and penance is meant to avert evil and war, but most of all to save souls." When the other visionaries were questioned about the sign, they said it will appear spontaneously in the sky and will be permanent and indestructible. According to Mirjana, the events predicted by the Blessed Virgin are near. By virtue of this knowledge, Mirjana proclaims to the world, "Convert as quickly as possible. Open your hearts to God."

One message given to Mirjana by the Virgin Mary was, "*Excuse me for this,* **but you must realize that Satan exists**. *One day he appeared before the throne of God and asked permission to submit the church to a period of trial.* **God gave him permission to try the church for one century**. *This century is under the power of the devil, but when the secrets confided to you come to pass, his power will be destroyed. Even now he is beginning to lose his power and has become aggressive.* **He is destroying marriages,** *creating division among priests and* **is responsible for obsessions and murder. You must protect yourselves against these things through fasting** *and* **prayer**, *especially community prayer. Carry blessed objects with you. Put them in your house, and restore the use of holy water.*

Each visionary is to receive ten secrets, but it is not known whether all ten secrets are the same. In fact the visionaries do not know each other's secrets. Currently three visionaries (Mirjana, Ivanka, and Jakov) have already received ten secrets, but once each visionary has received all ten secrets; it is anticipated that it will initiate the last days. The three visionaries that have been given all ten secrets no longer see Our Lady on a daily basis; they only see her on special occasions like their birthday.

The six visionaries are humble and patient, they have spoken to tens of thousands of people, while living plain and ordinary lives. Imagine what it is like for them to be constantly asked the same questions a thousand times. How many individuals would remain patient with people after being asked the same question even a couple dozen times? Some of them have traveled throughout the world speaking to people about their experience and generally, the Virgin Mary will appear to the visionary during that moment. In many instances, after the visionary had spoken to the Holy Mother, he will give a message to those present during her appearance.

At Medjugorje, pilgrims of many faiths and some nonbelievers have attended the mass and parish at which these apparitions occur. Many have had soul altering experiences and come around to believing in Mary's messages and presence there. Moreover many pilgrims have claimed to see the sun spinning with brilliant lights coming off it and furthermore there have been thousands of miracle healings. Why are so many miracles taking place? Why is the Virgin Mary trying so hard to change us?

Another aspect concerning the visionaries is that they have a sense of inner peace about themselves, and although they know the secrets, they do not fear the future. As the Blessed Mother has told all the visionaries over the past sixty years, those who convert and pray the Rosary with meditation will be protected by her and the angels at the end of time, so they need not fear.

Since 1987, the Blessed Mother has been giving a monthly message to the visionaries for the inhabitants of the world. This message is given on twenty-fifth day of the month and before conveying the message for the world, she appears to the visionaries and politely greets them, *"Dear children"*. When she is finished giving the message she says, *"thank you for having responded to my call."* In the beginning her messages, she was asking the people of the world to start living holy lives, to submit their will to God, and to establish a relationship with Jesus.

The early messages by the Virgin Mary, for the peoples of the world, were focused upon surrendering our wills to God, and it is apparent that unless this is accomplished, one remains vulnerable to the devil's influence; as a result many souls will be susceptible to him and fall into damnation. Those being misled are focused on fame, power, money, lust, material goods, popularity, self-gratification, etc. These things are like perishable food; they will not last. The real food for happiness cannot rot and comes from Heaven. Satan wants us to be fixated on the things on Earth and to give up our true inheritance of Heaven. This is the reason why he is trying so hard, and successfully, to have people enjoy the fruits of this world. They may taste sweet initially, but will become sour and bitter after placing it in our mouth.

The Blessed Virgin Mary's messages remind us that we are the children of God. We have to pray, pray, and pray not only to be protected from evil, but also for God's mercy, understanding, strength, and guidance in this world. Mary tells us that with prayer; we can stop wars, alter nature, and defeat Satan himself. All that is required of us is to submit our wills to God. Unfortunately, most people do not pray and seek out God; much like a drowning man that refuses to take in the thrown rope to be rescued; he ends up drowning. We too are like him when we refuse to pray to God and be rescued from evil. Mary continually warns us that Satan does exist and her messages are trying to keep us on the right path before it is too late.

As the messages progressed throughout the years, their focus became fixated on conversion. The direction of Mary's messages, point to the timeline in mankind's future that is rapidly approaching the end. The analogy would be as if the ship is ready to sink, and the captain is telling everyone to get to the life rafts before it is too late. By her calling us to conversion, she is saying this is our life raft, and in order not to drown in the sea of sin, we need to heed her advice. If we do not convert, then we will be tested and have to suffer more than any other generation. Our greed, malice, depravations, licentiousness, immorality, hatred, anger, etc. will be the cause for this suffering. Our penance will require us to experience the pain, hurt, suffering that we inflicted upon others in this world.

In addition to the messages given to believers, Mary has been giving special messages on the second day of each month that are directed towards non-believers. Throughout the 1990s there were only two messages for them, but now the Virgin Mary is giving monthly messages for non-believers. What would prompt her to start giving monthly messages for non-believers, unless the time for them to convert is quickly falling away? She is asking them to choose her Son now, and live the message of God. How many times does she need to ask people to convert, to change, to accept God, and still she is being ignored? If we ignore her then our souls could end up in Hell or if we a lucky, end up in Purgatory instead.

Several of the Medjugorje visionaries were physically taken in body; by the Virgin Mary, to Heaven, Purgatory, and Hell. Vicka described Hell as a place where "in the center of it there is a great fire, like an ocean of raging flames. We could see **people** before they **went into the fire**, and then we could see them coming out of the fire. Before they go into the fire, they look like normal people. The more they are against God's will, the deeper they enter into the fire, and the deeper they go, the more they rage against Him. **When they come out of the fire, they don't have human shape anymore**; they are more like grotesque animals, but unlike anything on Earth. It's as if they were never human beings before…They were horrible, ugly and angry. And each was different; no two looked alike…When they came out, they were raging and smashing everything around and hissing and gnashing and screeching"

Mirjana's description of Hell is "it's a large space with a big sea of fire in the middle. **There are many people there**. I particularly **noticed a beautiful young girl**, but when she came near the fire, she was no longer beautiful. **She came out of the fire like an animal; she was no longer human**." The Blessed Mother told me that God gives us all choices. Everyone responds to these choices. Everyone can choose if he wants to go to Hell or not. Anyone who goes to Hell chooses Hell.

One of the greatest tragedies in our world are people who are not bad people, but do not fully worship God. If an individual is fortunate enough not to go into Hell, but are not good enough to be in Heaven, then Purgatory is a place a soul will go to be purified. It is a place where we have to remove the stain caused by our sins. God requires nothing but purity of a soul before going into Heaven. It is like a mother telling her kids to take off those muddy shoes before going into the house; she doesn't want it messed up. There are apparently multiple levels of Purgatory and the worse of them goes very deep and requires a longer the time for a soul to be there before being released. The Blessed Mother showed the visionaries Purgatory, a real place that many religions do not recognize as existing.

Vicka described purgatory as "an endless space of ashy color. It was quite dark. I could feel people struggling and suffering there. The Blessed Mother told us we should be praying for souls stranded in Purgatory. She said only our prayers and sacrifices can release them from that place… The people there are helpless. They are really suffering. We can be like Jesus a little bit if we just do some voluntary penance for the souls in Purgatory; especially for the ones who are abandoned by their families on Earth…I am aware of their suffering. I know some of their torment. I know how desperately they need our prayers. They are so lonely that it is almost sickening to remember those moments I was there. It is really a great joy to do penance for the poor souls because I know how much it helps them… And many of our family members who have died desperately need our prayers. The Blessed Mother says we must pray courageously for them so that they might go to heaven. They are powerless to help themselves."

Mirjana's description of Purgatory is "There are **several levels in Purgatory**. The more you pray on Earth, the higher your level in Purgatory will be… **The lowest level is the closest to Hell**, where the **suffering is the most intense**. The highest level is closest to Heaven, and there the suffering is the least. What level you are on depends on the state of purity of your soul. The lower the level the people are on in Purgatory, the less they are able to pray and the more they suffer. The higher the level a person is in Purgatory, the easier it is for him to pray, the more he enjoys praying and the less he suffers… The Blessed Mother has asked us to pray for the souls in Purgatory. They are helpless to pray for themselves. Through prayer, we on Earth can do much to help them. The Blessed Mother told me that when most souls leave Purgatory and go to Heaven it is on Christmas Day."

The reward of conversion and obedience to God is great. God realizes that Satan is a powerful enemy and has the ability to makes us abandon God, by chasing the trivial things of this world. Many people do not know what paradise will be like, so they attempt to make Earth a paradise. It is a short lived-one and when death comes to them; they will have chosen their resting place for all of eternity through their choices on Earth. Hell has been described as a tortuous place, which does not acknowledge beauty, power, fame, or anything accomplished in this world. Only flames and sorrow is the everlasting fate for those who reject God. How many famous and wealthy people are currently in Hell forever? What good did their fame or wealth do? However, the converse is true for those who are obedient to God and the Blessed mother took or showed the visionaries heaven.

Vicka's response to the question on what Heaven looks like, "…it can't be described. That is something beyond description. It is filled with some sort of beautiful light…people…flowers…angels… All is filled with some indescribable joy. Your heart stands still when you look at it. Heaven is a vast space, and it has a brilliant light which does not leave it. It is a life which we do not know here on Earth. We saw people dressed in gray, pink, and yellow robes. They were walking, praying, and singing. Small angels were flying above them". The Blessed Mother showed us how happy these people are. You can see it on their faces. But it is impossible to describe with words the great happiness I saw in Heaven… In paradise, when the Blessed Mother passed, everybody responded to her, and she to them. There was recognition between them… They were standing there communicating with her, like in a tunnel, only it wasn't exactly like a tunnel, but a tunnel is the closest comparison. People were praying, they were singing, they were looking… People in Heaven know the absolute fullness of a created being."

Mirjana didn't physically go to Heaven, but saw it during one of her apparitions. She said, "I saw Heaven as if it were a movie. The first thing I noticed was the faces of the people there; they were radiating a type of inner light which showed how immensely happy they were. The **trees, meadows and the sky are totally**

different from anything we know on the Earth. And the light is much more brilliant. Heaven is beautiful beyond any possible comparison with anything I know of on the Earth. People have bodies in Heaven, but they were different from what we are like now. Perhaps they were all around thirty years of age… They were walking in a beautiful park. They have everything. They need or want nothing. They are totally full… They were dressed in the types of clothing that Jesus wore."

Marija's description of Heaven is "I had a vision of Heaven, like you watch a movie on screen or looking out a window. I wasn't actually there like the other visionaries… I have never seen such a picture before; no one can even begin to imagine how it looks…the people were around the flowers. They were all the same age. No one in Heaven is older than the age of Christ. People in Heaven were full of joy and all of them are giving thanks for the gifts given to them of God. Every day they realize how much love God has for them… There was a multitude of people."

The messages of Medjugorje are not like other visionary messages that describe the wrath of God is coming and to prepare for the chastisements. The messages of Medjugorje are in some sense much more terrifying in one way, but beautiful in another. The Blessed Mother asks us to convert now. Her messages are warning us that it is not business as usual; instead it is, "you are going to be out of business".

We all live in this world and go through suffering, but eventually we see that there is a purpose and an end to life. We all go through it; it is like being at the train depot to go on a destination and then the conductor calls out "all aboard". We have a choice to either enter that train leading us to Heaven, a place with trees, flowers and indescribable beauty, or ignore the call and end up in a place where there is nothing but flames, agony, and loneliness. It is our decision because the pot of water is already boiling and we have better be prepared for our eternal resting place.

Chapter 19

Tears

The loss (death) of someone special will bring tears into the eyes of surviving family members and friends. It is an experience that everyone feels in their lifetime. They know that they will never see that individual again in this world. It is no different for the Virgin Mary. She is the mother of all mankind and she knows what is going to become of humanity and even to Earth itself. It must be a very sorrowful moment for her to have knowledge of our future. Statues, paintings, prayer cards, and pictures depicting her, have exuded tears, oil, or blood. In some cases the tears and blood were contrived, but other cases the tears and blood were analyzed and found to be human. Even after the fluids had been wiped away from the statue, painting or picture; they would immediately exude more fluids. In many instances the fluids were collected in vials, and in some instances, they were found to cure various illnesses of people.

There have been over one hundred accounts of statues, pictures, and painting depicting Jesus or Mary crying either tears of blood or water. These accounts have come all over the world. The Vatican has taken these miraculous events seriously, and has determined some of them to be authentic, while some have been fabricated. Still many others are currently being investigated.

A statue of the Madonna, belonging to a Chilean woman named Olga Rodriguez, was found to be weeping blood from her eyes. The statue was analyzed by the Santiago police, Criminal Investigation Department, which had three samples of the red liquid examined in a laboratory. The results came back to be type O-4 negative human blood.

In 1995, a statue of Jesus in Bolivia was found to weep, and seep blood from the wounds caused by the crown of thorns. The blood was analyzed by a laboratory, not knowing of its origin, and they found it to be human origin. During the transit of the sample, a scab-like substance had broken off. The substance was analyzed by forensic scientists, who found the particle to be the tip of a vicious thorn or spine. They concluded that the thorn could have only come from an arid region containing date palms or hawthorn bushes. Both of which are not located in Bolivia.

The Vatican has evaluated and approved a weeping statue known as Our Lady of Akita. The statue had cried tears 101 times between the years 1973-1980, but has since stopped crying. In other cases, there have been paintings of the Virgin Mary that have wept so much, the tears made a stain trail through the incessant tearing. In some cases, the tears have been reported to perform miraculous healings.

There have been many other reports of statues weeping. So many tears are being shed for humanity by super natural phenomena. There may be tears of blood for all the people who will suffer; tears of sadness for those who have rejected God and perhaps tears of oil for the healing. On February 20, 2005, a group of people who were praying in a grotto noticed the aroma of perfume oil. When they went to investigate the odor, they found a little statue of Jesus in the Garden of Gethsemane oozing the perfumed substance. At the same time, the large cross of Jesus started to flow with the oil from the head and the wounds on the side.

On February 28, 2004, a photo was taken by Fr. James Manjackal rHere showing a statue of the Mother of god weeping tears in the room of missionary Carmen Patricia. The statue had a life-like sadness about its appearance and has continued to weeps tears. In 1996, in Lewis, Kansas, an image of Our Lady of Guadalupe owned by Margarita Holguin was found to be weeping tears one day; the following day the tears had turned to blood. In 1998, in Las Vegas, NV, the backyard shrine of Pablo Covarrubias contained a statue of the Virgin of Guadalupe that was found to regularly weep real tears. They are harvested in little cotton balls and distributed to the faithful.

In 1992, A Catholic parish priest in Lake Ridge, Virginia found statues of the Virgin Mary weeping tears and/or blood.

Other statues on the parish grounds have been seen to weep as well. In 1992, in Santiago, Chile, a six-inch-high porcelain statue of the Virgin Mary wept tears of blood. The red liquid staining the image has been verified as human blood, Type O-Positive. In 1999, in Bolivia, Katya Revas found a statue of Mary weeping blood at times and tears of oil at other times. The blood was tested and found to be that of a woman.

On February 15, 1996, a statue of Our Lady of Lourdes in a Carmelite Sisters' convent in Diego Martin, West Trinidad, began weeping tears of blood. When the blood was tested, it was found to be of human origin. One Sunday, in June 1994 at Rincon, Puerto Rico, churchgoers at the Santa Rosa de Lima church saw tears falling from the cheek of the Virgin Mary statue. The tears came regularly from the statue's left eye and rolled down her cheek to her neck.

In 1994, in Grangecon, Ireland, a statue of the Madonna, whose eyes were initially filled with tears, proceeded to weep blood that trickled from the from her left eye leaving a brown stain on the statue. In 1995, in the tiny Southern Ireland village of Grangecon, County Wicklow, a 12- inch statue of the Virgin Mary, sealed in a glass case, was found to cry blood that stained the cheeks of the statue. In 1998, in the quiet village of Mura, Spain, a local priest Luis Costa discovered a 28-inch tall white-marble Madonna statue appeared to be crying tears of blood from one corner of each eye. Analysis showed that the blood had partially coagulated.

In 1994, in Sydney, Australia, a sixteen-year-old boy found a small statue of Our Lady of Fatima weeping tears. The statue wept so many tears that the owners of the statue needed to place cotton balls between the lady's praying hands and her body to collect the moisture. In 1994, a bas-relief of the Holy Virgin in Tivoli, east of Rome, began weeping tears. In another part of Italy at Taranta Peligna, a statue that was purchased at Lourdes, developed bloodstains on its face, throat, breasts, and hands. Nearby in a village called Castrovillari, a weeping statue of the Virgin Mary was found to weep tears of blood. When the blood was analyzed it was found to be human, belonging to the O-positive blood group.

In 1995, in Civitavecchia, Italy a statue of the Virgin Mary wept tears of blood. The statue was brought back to Italy from Medjugorje for a family whose son suffered from poor health. The tears of blood have been analyzed by Vatican scientific experts and have been found to be the blood from a male. In 1995, a statue of the Virgin Mary, purchased at Medjugorje was taken to the village of Civitavecchia, Italy where it began to weep tears of blood. In 1997, a theological commission appointed by the Vatican analyzed and accepted it, as a miracle.

The numbers of reported weeping statues have grown disproportionately large since the 1970s. Although, some have been faked, there appears to be a greater number that are authentic. Many of these weeping icons, statues, or pictures have yet to be completely investigated by the Vatican. Assuming these weeping icons are a message from God, it must be one of great importance. Why would God lament so much, unless some unprecedented earth-shattering event is about to take place in our near future? Some critics would say these bleeding images took place back in the 1970s and 1990s, and if God was going to annihilate the world, why hasn't he done it? We must remember from Thessalonians 1 (5:2), "*But of the times and the seasons, brethren, ye have no need that I write unto you. For yourselves know perfectly that the day of the Lord so cometh as a thief in the night. For when they shall say, Peace and safety; then sudden destruction cometh upon them, as travail upon a woman with child; and they shall not escape. But ye, brethren, are not in darkness, that that day should overtake you as a thief. Ye are all the children of light, and the children of the day: we are not of the night, nor of darkness.*"

The bleeding statues, the apparitions and messages of Mary, the events at Fatima and Medjugorje are all derived from God, as attempts to call us back to Him. Although we do not know the day or the hour, we should always be prepared for that moment when it will happen.

Epilogue

There is no question that the world is rapidly coming to an end. Just look around and see all the atrocities and tragedies occurring in our daily lives; as testament to that which was prophesized long ago. In addition, look at the facts and messages received by visionaries given to them by the Virgin Mary. All of which have been presented in the interior of this book. Many people will never accept the concept that our world is on course to experience its' last days within our lifetime. They will continue living amoral lives; however, on judgment day they will be the ones outside the gates trying to get in to Heaven, but shall be denied.

No one truly knows the 'exact hour or date' the world will end, except God, although the signs in today's world clearly show that humanity is on a zenith of this transformation. The world can no longer go on as business as usual. There are too many disparities between the haves and have not's and the world is about to erupt. As resources become fewer and fewer, the have not's will resent those who have, and perhaps out of this suffering will come the antichrist. History teaches us that economic and social disparities often give rise to evil; such as, Adolf Hitler's rise to power in Germany.

If we feel that the end times are near, they can be altered, just as they did in Nineveh by praying and fasting. If enough people prayed to God; especially saying the Rosary with meditation on the mysteries, it could be enough to stop the chastisements. If not, those who pray the Rosary have been insured by the Virgin Mary's promise of protection in these last days. It is up to each individual, whether they believe, or not, in the power of prayer.

For those individuals who doubt in the existence of God and the apparitions of the Virgin Mary; they will be the first ones who say, "I was a fool for not believing". The Blessed Mother said there is only so much time to convert and once the permanent sign appears in the sky, it will be too late. It is imperative for people to amend their lifestyles. Go to church and stop blaspheming God, stop stealing, stop lying, stop fornicating, stop doing drugs, stop killing, stop being greedy, stop hating, stop all things offensive to God. If you don't, you will suffer from His wrath on Earth and perhaps suffer an eternity in Hell where there is no love, no hope of reprieve; nothing but an eternity of slavery to Satan. In Hell, all you beautiful men and women will become grotesque beast, there will be no smiles on your face, nothing to drink, nothing to eat, no mansions, no friends, no rest, no joy, no happiness, only misery and pain for ever.

Many people cannot comprehend how long eternity is. An idea to its length can be compared to the age of the universe, which formed eight billion years ago, but in contrast to eternity; that amount of passing has not even scratched the surface of time. For sinners, their suffering in Hell will be like that amount of time passed since creation of the universe, in that it is only the beginning. It is important they open their hearts to the Holy Spirit before Jesus's return. It may be only five years from now, it may be less and it may be today if they die. Time is not on the side for sinners.

CPSIA information can be obtained at www.ICGtesting.com
Printed in the USA
LVOW07s1419250116

472157LV00001BA/95/P